ORGANICITY

Praise for Organicity: Entropy or Evolution

"Urban design now recognises the need for alternatives to soulless and dispiriting residential developments located far from jobs, schools, shops, leisure and social opportunities. There is a rising awareness, too, that in its quest for short-term returns, conventional speculative property development passes onto communities the long-term risks of biodiversity loss, social fragmentation, environmental degradation, energy and transport costs, and more. Explored here is a prototype for an alternative model to residential development that puts holistic resilience and sustainability first. In these compact 'urban cells,' cars have been designed out. Work is local and self-sufficiency in power, water, and food is possible. Social cohesion is allowed to emerge. Importantly, the financial instruments needed to seed and grow such communities already exist."

— Paul Jones, an award-winning British architect and professor at Northumbria University. He is a Principal Fellow of the Higher Education Academy (HEA), an active member of the Royal Institute of British Architects (RIBA) and a member of the Standing Council of Heads of Schools of Architecture (SCHOSA).

"David Dobereiner is an architect who has turned successfully to philosophy to help him to reflect on his plentiful and myriad life experiences, as well as to guide those of others. Organicity is a thoughtful and provocative book that flits through a wide range of fields, including climate science, biology, the philosophy of mind, and political theory. The result is a plea for human beings to lead more grounded lives wherein they take more personal responsibility, engage more and differently with their local communities (for example, in weekly assemblies), and restore the pleasure from establishing more meaningful contacts with others, including the lives of nonhumans... Dobereiner is a truly free spirit who never hesitates to say what he thinks, regardless

Praise for Organicity: Entropy or Evolution

of what other people make of it... The book is inspirational for those who are concerned with many social and ecological problems of our 'Machinic' age, including health and wealth inequalities, pollution, climate change, and soil degradation. I commend the book highly to anyone who is interested in seeking a much needed alternative to current world chaos."

— Jan Deckers, Senior Lecturer in Bioethics at Newcastle University and author of *Animal (De)Liberation*

"The culmination of a life's thought and care for nature, Organicity: Entropy or Evolution is a searching diagnosis of how we became mired in environmental crisis and a passionate demand for change which takes heed of the mistakes of the past. An anarchist, architect, philosopher, and environmentalist, Dobereiner weaves together his commitments in a book bristling with ideas that resists classification. In dialogue, interview, manifesto, letters, and philosophical analysis, it is a book by turns political, psychological, historical, economical, autobiographical, and one in which the reader is not surprised to find Deleuze, Jane Goodall, and Vandana Shiva together on one page. [Emerging from] his visionary ecological urban design work (Dobereiner is an architect by profession), the concept of Organicity is a fascinating conception of a future way of life that seeks to enable the social and environmental changes required to establish a sustainable model in which nature can flourish.

"Organicity is unflinching in its survey of our predicament but it reflects deeply not only on where we have gone wrong but also shares an imaginative vision of how things can be done, have to be done, differently."

— Alan Shepherd is a freelance writer and MA graduate from the Department of Philosophy at the University of Glasgow.

ORGANICITY

ENTROPY OR EVOLUTION

DAVID DOBEREINER

BLACK ROSE BOOKS

Montréal/Chicago/London

Black Rose Books No. T400

Library and Archives Canada Cataloguing in Publication

Title: Organicity : entropy or evolution / David Dobereiner.
Names: Dobereiner, David, author.
Identifiers: Canadiana (print) 20190080914 | Canadiana (ebook) 20190080973 | ISBN 9781551647289 (softcover) | ISBN 9781551647265 (hardcover) | ISBN 9781551647302 (PDF)
Subjects: LCSH: Sustainable development.
Classification: LCC HC79.E5 D63 2019 | DDC 338.9/27—dc23

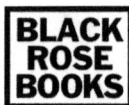

BLACK ROSE BOOKS

C.P.35788 Succ. Léo-Pariseau
Montréal, QC, H2X 0A4
Canada

Explore our books and subscribe to our newsletter:
www.blackrosebooks.com

Ordering Information

USA/INTERNATIONAL	CANADA	UK/IRELAND
University of Chicago Press Chicago Distribution Center 11030 South Langley Avenue Chicago, IL 60628	University of Toronto Press 5201 Dufferin Street Toronto, ON M3H 5T8	Central Books 50 Freshwater Road Chadwell Heath, London RM8 1RX
(800) 621-2736 (USA) (773) 702-7000 (International) orders@press.uchicago.edu	1-800-565-9523 utpbooks@utpress.utoronto.ca	+44 (0) 20 8525 8800 contactus@centralbooks.com

Black Rose Books is a not-for-profit publishing project of Cercle Noir et Rouge

TABLE OF CONTENTS

For Nancy

PREFACE

In the beginning was organi-CITY. After I retired as an architect, it morphed into organ-IC-ity. But they are the same thing, however pronounced.

Let me explain. During my training as an architect I discovered the concept of Organic Architecture. Later I began to think about the application of this concept to the city. Now the primary 'organs' of a city are (or should be) its residential neighbourhoods.[1]

Already in the early 60's, I had started to identify the nightmarish consequences of the unreflective pursuit of the American Dream. But it took me 40 years to publish my cure for that international trauma, now evident in major cities, world-wide.

Urban sprawl was a direct consequence of the capitalist economic system.

As soon as widespread car ownership made flight from the city to the country possible, the hollowing out of urban society began.

One consequence was the suburbs, a vast area that was neither city nor country but something in between that lacked the benefits of easy access to urban facilities while at the same time destroying the advantages for individual families of living amongst greenery.

The other consequence was the deterioration of conditions in urban slums. Slums were what made the middle class want to get away from the city, and they did. They wanted to look out of their windows and see trees. Instead, they looked out of their windows and saw other people looking out of their windows at them.

But many now owned cars and houses when they had previously not needed them.

This was profitable for manufacturers, developers and bankers but not for the people who had bought into the system (or anyone else).

For a period of three and a half years I ran a group with the Newcastle Philosophy Society. It met every month in my flat. I wrote a lecture to kick off the discussion at each meeting. Each chapter of this book roughly corresponds to each successive lecture although the form of the lecture varies.

One chapter is a play, another a letter, another a list. Some are conventional in length and some are much shorter. All this was to add variety and to stimulate discussion in my 'course.'

Science has largely replaced Religion in the modern world in terms of providing a narrative that most people believe comes closest to the relevant truths. And science, ever since Descartes, has been dominated by an assumption, that the universe can be fully explained by the laws of physics and chemistry.

But ever since Newton, the laws of physics have proved inadequate to explain even the most basic aspects of the material world before we even begin to examine its mental attributes. Newton, who proved that 'action at a distance' was omnipresent as the force of gravity, was puzzled by his own discovery. Something else was needed to explain the physical reality, something invisible, untouchable, and ostensibly non-existent except that gravity cannot be explained without positing its existence. This was the gravitational field, only independently confirmed to exist in recent years.

Quantum electrodynamics suggests that some physical phenomena somehow 'exist,' but not in space/time, like everything else we know. Space/time itself is a hard concept for ordinary people to get their head around. Did anyone but Einstein himself really grasp what he meant by the 'curvature' of space/time?

It can be explained mathematically but not intuitively.

In the same way the machine technology starting up at the end of the 18th century depended on the old scientific credo of cause and effect. If scientists had been at the stage they are now, thinking much more holistically, they would perhaps have warned the inventors to think about the long-term side-effects of burning fossil fuels. Then James Watt might have delayed introducing his steam engine until after he had found a way of decarbonizing the smoke of burned coal. It might have prevented the major health disaster of London air pollution a century later, and the existential threat of global climate breakdown today.

Spirit =
Holy Spirit =
God's Will =
The Ineffable=
The Numinous=
The Tao =
Buddhism's Ninth Consciousness=
Freud's Unconscious Mind =
Jung's Collective Unconscious =
Bergson's Élan Vital=
Reich's Orgone Energy Pool =
Sheldrake's Morphic/Morphogenic Field =
Panpsychism=
Organicity =
You Name It

Seen from the perspective of different cultures and sub-cultures the same essence is given different names. Why then, did I need to invent a new name? The answer is partly what this book is about.

Notes

[1]   *The End of the Street: Sustainable Growth within Natural Limits–Black Rose Books 2006.*

INTRODUCTION

THE WAY TO STOP ECOCIDE

Human animals are born of Mother Earth. How come we attack her so violently?[2]

This is the first question.

Human animals are all siblings in the same Earth Nest. How come we attack each other so violently?[3]

This is the second question.

It is the thesis of Organicity that these questions have a common answer:

The dominance of Dominance (or Patriarchy).

Whence came dominance and how did it come to dominate? This is easily answered.

Humans are naked apes, ill-equipped to survive in the wild. We have no built-in weapons or tools, such as dagger-like teeth, sharp claws or wings. We are also physically weak by comparison with any competitors of equivalent mass. All we have is an outsized brain.

That was enough, (combined with the gift of language, brought about by a chance mutation, that, by natural selection was rapidly spread among the human population)[4] to enable our kind to learn how to control fire, to clothe, shelter, and to defend ourselves. With our stone tipped weapons, we achieved parity with other animals. Populations remained small and stable but life was short. We, as yet, did not have the power to damage or disrupt the ecosystems in which we were embedded.

Then we committed the Original Sin. We invented agriculture.[5]

We claimed the right to cordon off an area of the commons (common to all creatures), to select organisms we wished to use, and to kill off or expel those we had no use for. One species appropriated land and dominated everything it chose to allow to live on it.

One species, for the first time, instead of adapting to the habitat in which it had evolved, as do all other species[6], started to create its own *separate* habitat, shared with a few others, on sufferance.

And this was extremely successful for humanity, especially in the great river valleys of the temperate zone. For the first time, families could produce more food than they could eat. This surplus food could then be appropriated by another class of person, a non-producing person, the aristocrat.

Two regimes of dominance were thereby instituted. Man, over nature and Man over Man, to put it briefly.[7] Why Man, and not Woman? Because the urge to dominate is the predominant male trait, is it not?

Certainly, the male's urge to fight another male in order to win access to a female, goes deep into natural history. Contrariwise, the almost complete absence of the urge to dominate and control among the females of many species is equally apparent.

Dominance came to dominate because it worked. Or so men thought.

༺༻

To return to the first two questions above. It may be objected that in the case of ecocide the situation is an unintended consequence whereas in the case of warfare, the major cause of violent death, it is waged intentionally by the aggressive leaders (nearly always male) who dominate and control imperialistic states.

There is a factor that unites the two. It is *collateral effects.*

Sadly, history shows that innovations in technology have usually been developed for military purposes primarily. Investing in better ways to kill human beings has produced many of the collateral benefits we have come to enjoy. A current example is the drone. It enables an imperialist power centered on one continent to assassinate an individual on another by purely mechanical and electronic means. That the individual in question usually has his innocent family simultaneously obliterated is dismissed as *collateral damage*. But the knowledge of how to give flying machines enough artificial intelligence to fly by remote control is, in itself, a valuable addition to knowledge. It is a *collateral benefit*.

The whole impact of the global economy on the global ecosystem can be seen as massive collateral damage. It was not planned, not intended, but it happened, is happening. And our growth-fixated mind set, along with the mighty engine of the free market that it has brought into being, seems incapable of self-correcting. It blunders on, like a huge machine with no driver in control ... except ... the Market?[8]

Some of the technological by-products of the military industrial complex have contributed enormously to the growth of the already (locally) over-grown civilian economy. We welcome these benefits because they seem to enrich our lives—which they do—at a cost of the further impoverishment of the planet: for example, the Internet.[9]

❧

Let us deconstruct the phrase 'Man over Nature.'

The word 'Man' in this context is understood to mean: all the men, women and children living in the world together with future generations of same—the human species—as distinct from other species.

The word 'Nature' is meaningless without qualification. The qualification implied in this context is the earthly biosphere as it is, minus the human species. This is an abstraction, since humans are, in reality, part of nature, and, from the human perspective, the most important part. If we were really subtracted what was left would be very different from what it is.

The word 'over' means in this context 'on top of' or 'above' in the same sense that the Master is above the Slave. The reference here is to domination, control, ownership, or use.

℘

There is an ethic of use that is generally accepted in all present-day cultures, as follows: use is morally neutral when predicated by a subject to an object. For a subject to use another subject is always wrong. A system that 'subjects' one class of subject to use by another is an immoral system; e.g. Master/Slave.

But cultures differ as to what they consider to be subjects. Ancient cultures denied subject-hood to slaves. Some religious and philosophical traditions classify non-human animals as merely objects or machines.

In these post-Darwin days such positions seem completely untenable. Any life form that is not rooted in the earth must move itself purposefully, in order to survive, feed, defend itself, and above all to reproduce.[10] You can't do these things without a will to do them. This implies, at some level, consciousness. Indeed, it implies an unconscious mind too, since it has been proved that animals have, and need, memory. If they didn't, they would instantly forget that they had offspring for whom they are responsible. Forgetful species would have been rooted out by natural selection.

If we accept as a natural moral law: 'subject shall not use[11] subject,' we see that it applies generally but is conditional on the level of awareness. It is possible that the lion is not aware of the subject-hood of the wildebeest she kills. Or if she is, may feel sorry for the prey but sees no alternative way (like Margaret Thatcher) of feeding her young. But big predators are relatively rare life forms. The ratio of herbivores to carnivores in the wild is approximately 1000 to 1.

Our human awareness has grown over the centuries. But we have not yet taken the next natural step of bestowing the same rights (to life, liberty and the pursuit of happiness) on non-human conscious beings as we accord, at least nominally, on ourselves. There has been talk of it. Human rights have been proposed for orangutans, dolphins and whales, for example.

∾

There is a sense in which the industrial revolution was a backward step for humankind. Natural forces of wind, water-flow, and muscle power were largely given up in favor of bio-chemical concentrations of energy beneath the earth's surface. These were favored over naturally occurring energy sources. It seemed they could be tapped at will and reliably supply any quantity needed. They possessed enormously enhanced energy density. Two hundred years later we discover there are life-threatening side-effects to fossil fuel exploitation and their supply is running out. Hence scientists are trying to find ways to replace fossil fuel use with scientific exploitation of some of the naturally occurring energies that were abandoned at the beginning, as well as others, such as sunlight.

During the same period, machines, machine made artifacts, and machine thinking came to dominate human life. If we look around us in our typical homes, we will see nothing hand-crafted, except perhaps the occasional child's school project. The pre-industrial condition, where everything was made by hand by specialized craftsmen is gone forever.

That was a time when, through the guild system, the making of objects, the transfer of objects to those who needed them, and the use of them, all these processes were knitted into the fabric of everyday life, and mediated through face to face contact between people who often knew each other. The ethic of the 'just price' ensured that crafted objects were valued at a rate that ensured a decent life for the guild members but no more.

Such systems, in which the necessities of life are more or less peacefully distributed to subjects of the same species on a more or less equal basis, are pervasive in nature. Subjects of the same species, occupying the same space, will default to an ethic of tolerance, tending to friendliness, rather than fighting. Fighting is too expensive (energy intensive).

The establishment of pecking orders does not contradict this principle but reinforces it. They are evolved to allow more conflict-free distribution of scarce goods. Within the local group, adult animals tend to behave decently to each other. As with human beings though, these behaviors are learned. Fledgling chicks of some bird species can be brats, ill-mannered, and unkind to their patient long suffering mothers. The ruling principle though, is not survival of the fittest—implying the death of the less fit, but 'live and let live' as peacefully as possible.

Intra-specific fighting and killing would have long since doomed any species that practiced it, to extinction. Consequently, it is rarely observed in the wild.

It seems that alongside the inventory of mankind's inventions we must include murder, torture and genocidal warfare.[12]

⟡

The suggestion here is that the intra-specific right to life is a principle deeply embedded in the 'lived world,'[13] and, if we are now re-asserting it, the only change is that, with our enhanced *human* awareness, we are morally obliged to apply it to the whole biosphere, composed of all the other species who each apply it instinctively to their own kind but cannot see other species as anything but 'the other.' But we, uniquely, can.[14]

⟡

The Organic is shorthand for the global eco-system. It is a complex system of organisms connecting with other organisms and the environment that sustains them. Its stability is partly dependent on its diversity, allowing greater resilience in the face of catastrophic events. Although it is only partly understood, certain underlying principles have been identified.

It is cyclic and self-regulating. Atmospheric content is naturally balanced due to plant life absorbing carbon dioxide producing oxygen, which is inhaled by animals who exhale the carbon dioxide that the plants need. Top soil, which feeds plants, is naturally enriched by decaying matter from the excreta of animals and the dead remains of all above ground life forms. The plants in turn feed the animals.

Through the cycles of procreation, birth, life and death, species are continuously evolved and created through mutations and the operation of natural selection. The Organic never repeats itself exactly. Even the leaves on the same tree are all different when observed in detail. The more complex the organism the more unique are the individuals found to be. Different personality traits have been observed even in worms. The Organic abhors Platonism and doctrines of perfection. In its place it valorizes infinite variety and endless flux—but not chaos.

The Organic can never be controlled or predicted because it is motivated by the will of its innumerable subjects—acting, ultimately, for the common good. Why this is so is not known and is perhaps unknowable.

The geometry of the Organic is the irregular and open-ended Helix.

Its guiding principle is Mystery.

The Machinic is shorthand for the non-Organic.

The geometry of the Machinic is the closed box.

Its ruling principle is Mastery.

✎

How, and at what point in time, the Machinic emerged from the Organic is mysterious, that is, itself, pertaining to the guiding principle of the Organic. Perhaps it emerged during the brief episode between the arrival of Homo Sapiens and the invention of language. Language was the first human tool. It was the master tool from which all subsequent moves for control of nature by humanity took off.

Be that as it may, language, as the tool for precise thinking in human heads that it became, was a radically new thing under the sun.

Out of Eros, Logos. Out of Logos, Logic. Out of Logic, Reason. And here there was a split—between Instrumental Reason and Disengaged Reason.[15]

If you start out with the mind-set that nothing in the universe matters, is important, or even truly exists, except the set of the human mind, you are already headed for the ecological crisis we are experiencing now. But it was this 17th century Cartesian mind-set that prevailed through the 18th century, spawned Humanism and was still widely subscribed to during the formative years of the Industrial Revolution of the early 19th Century.

The first machines were the by-product of impressive gains in the sciences of physics and chemistry following through from pioneering work by Galileo and others.

These were empiricists who believed in the evidence of their senses and who created theories to account for them using instrumental reason. The rhetoric and mythos of science created the comforting image of linear progression toward truth.

Among the earliest machines were those used in the cotton industry in Manchester. By assembling women in a factory and making them work long hours at numerous identical spinning and weaving machines, enormous productivity gains were made. And, of course, profits for the owners, the capitalists.

Several seminal institutions were pioneered here, that remain with us to this day, and that changed forever the pre-industrial world. Among these institutions—new ways of exploiting and degrading women—by Patriarchy.

The word Machinic embraces not only machines themselves, but all the tools, appliances, computers and gadgets that comprise the contemporary developed world.

It includes not only the machines themselves but everything that is machine made.

Not only those, but the factories that produce them are also Machinic. The system of mass production itself is in a sense the essence of the Machinic.

The logic of the Machinic is that it tends to ever increased size. Even without Capitalism, the efficiency of factory production would follow the law: *quantity* is inversely proportional to unit cost.

With Capitalism, that is to say under the rubric of the 'free market paradigm,' so universally accepted now, profits can be increased by increasing production at a higher rate than unit cost to the consumer is lowered.[16]

This is one of the reasons for the high degree of centralization of material production that has occurred. Essentially, all the goods and even some of the services reaching the developing, developed. and over-developed parts of the world are now produced in one region of the globe—China and SE Asia—in factories of ever-increasing size.

Since for the Organic, *small is beautiful,* we have a major conflict, because the Machinic's, watchword is, *the bigger the better.*

∽

It is the thesis of Organicity, that to the degree human organisms are liberated from entanglement in Machinic institutions, and returned to small self-regulating communities of human scale, both in the neighborhood and the workplace, we will be able to slow down the Machinic juggernaut sufficiently to save the planet.

It is also asserted that only such a turn to the natural laws of the Organic will bring us naturally to an embrace and new evaluation of the other animals we now recognize as organisms related to, and in many ways like, ourselves. This in turn will lead us to prioritize the repair and resuscitation of our common earthly home.[17]

Notes

[2] *The earth is 4.6 billion years old. Scaling to 46 years, we've been here 4 hours. The industrial revolution began 1 minute ago. In that time, we've destroyed 50% of the world's forests.*

[3] *By Fars News Agency, June 19, 2012 – TEHRAN (FNA) – The Iranian, Russian, Chinese and Syrian armies are due to stage joint amphibious exercises along the Syrian coasts in coming weeks, informed sources revealed on Monday. According to informed sources, 90,000 forces from the four countries will take part in the land and sea war games due to be held in Syria.*

[4] *Other animals vocalize and communicate but only the human is born with the rules of grammar and syntax, combined with the physiological attributes necessary for precise communication of thoughts and feelings related to both real and abstract entities, according to Chomsky.*

[5] *Or so we thought. Actually, ants had invented it billions of years earlier.*

[6] *With few exceptions. Dolphins create artificial bubble nets and again, one sub species of ant are agriculturalists.*

[7] *For this notion I am, of course, completely indebted to the late Murray Bookchin.*

[8] *'The efforts of governments are concentrated not on defending the living Earth from destruction, but on defending the machine that is destroying it. Whenever consumer capitalism becomes snarled up by its own contradictions, governments scramble to mend the machine, to ensure——though it consumes the conditions that sustain our lives— that it runs faster than ever before.' George Monbiot*

[9] *How so? The Internet has already had and is set to continue having enormous effects, mostly good. But in our market society it is*

inevitable that it is used to increase GNP globally. And we are at a turning point where growth under 'business as usual' is the last thing we need.

10　*Natural selection seems inadequate, by itself, to explain why any animal would bother to use so much energy to find a suitable mate, build and defend a nest, procreate and nurture its young. Genetics gets us nowhere. Bergson's 'élan vitale' is perhaps nearer the mark. They do it because the want to. They love to do it.*

11　*Killing, for the purpose of eating, is on the one hand the most egregious form of use. On the other hand, perhaps the most justifiable—in cases where the alternative is starvation and death of the killer.*

12　*The infanticide of male lions who displace a rival male is an anomalous exception, not the norm. The territorial battles between chimpanzee tribes observed by Jane Goodall were horrific but not genocidal.*

13　*The 'lived world' is an expression I have borrowed from De Leuze and Guattari in 'What is Philosophy' but I intend it to be understood as including all conscious subjects, not just humans.*

14　*'This is the last contest between a life destroying world view of Man's Empire over the Earth and a life protecting world view of harmony with nature, and recognition of the Rights of Mother Earth. I carried 100,000 signatures from India for the Universal Declaration on the Rights of Mother Earth which were handed over to the UN secretary General Ban Ki Moon.' – Vandana Shiva at Rio +20.*

15　*Descartes's wrong belief that we can only reach truth by disengaging the mind from the material world, including the reality of our own body and its urges, laid the ground work for the fatal move of humanity away from its Earth Mother to the Machinic.*

16　*There are other reasons that endless growth is indissolubly linked to the essential nature of our global economic system but these will be expanded on later in this book.*

17　*The proper purpose of the Machinic is to produce objects in the service of human subjects. To the extent that at present this production system entails the enslavement of human subjects, progress ought to be defined as replacing those enslaved, with robots, thus freeing those subjects to rejoin their comrades in the Organic.*

CHAPTER 1

ORGANICITY IN A NUTSHELL

Aristotle, in his History of Animals, writes: *'Man, by the way, presents a mixture of the two characters, the gregarious and the solitary.'*

Today it is commonplace to assert that humans, as social animals, naturally seek out and enjoy the company of others. Less commonly is this coupled with our other side, the need for solitude, or privacy, at times.

The philosophy of British empiricism (Locke, Berkeley, Hume and the Utilitarians), propelled parts of the world in three different directions.

In America, the path led from the classical liberalism of Adam Smith to the neo-liberalism of Milton Friedman and F. A. Hayek. This path emphasized freedom of the individual above all other values. Equality and fraternity were not considered desirable or necessary.[18] This path seems to have led to freedom's opposite, the hegemony of a few billionaires who have bought everything, including the vast majority of the people's representatives in government.

The second path, influenced by continental philosophy, led towards Owenite socialism and Marxist communism. As practiced in Russia and China, this path prioritized fraternity. It rejected freedom because it was a despised bourgeois value, and equality because it would have negated the dictatorship of the proletariat. A dictator, even a collective one, must have something to dictate to, a punching bag. At last, fraternity too fell by the wayside, within the Communist Party itself, where the party line was imposed ruthlessly by one man, and even more so as between the party and the people. Trust and empathy, which are the basis of fraternity, evaporated in a violent cauldron of mutual suspicion and fear. The result was Stalinism, indistinguishable in practice from its ideological opposite, Fascism.

The third path, places equal value on freedom, equality, and fraternity. It recognizes that the three aims are inseparable. Any one pursued to the exclusion of the other two will end up losing all three. They are the foundations of any good society.

John Stuart Mill called this ideal system libertarian socialism.

At first, freedom seems to differ from the other two in that it is personal whereas equality and fraternity are social. On second thoughts, we reflect that fulfilling our deepest desires, which is what freedom is, *always* involves at least one other person.[19] So all three goods are social, in the end.

Equality does not mean mathematical identity but a rough equivalence of access to whatever goods society offers. No one, anywhere on earth, should receive less than what they need to live a decent life. Above this level, goods become luxuries, responding to wants not needs. Ideally, anyone who bids for the allocation of luxury goods beyond the norm needs to justify themselves to the fraternity, and receive their consent by majority vote, or better still, consensus.

But at this moment, there is no fraternity. Fraternity (in its second meaning, the state or feeling of friendship and mutual support within a group) exists here and there in modern society but only in fragmentary and non-operative situations, for the most part.[20]

The global conversion to a faith in free markets, and American style neo-liberalism, has allowed technology to transform the world, improving the quality of life for many and lengthening it. On the other hand, it has dealt a death blow to any semblance of equality and fraternity.

The world would be an immensely happy place if the single global economy was broken up into a myriad of human scale autonomous communities, each living according to its own mores, evolved through its own process in general assembly.

The same spirit of fraternal mutual aid, because it would be honored within each community would then prevail also between communities, with the stronger naturally assisting the weaker economies.

Such an arrangement would maximize cultural diversity while tending towards an equalizing of the wherewithal to lead a good life, as between the presently rich north and the poor south, for example.

❧

The pattern of good social relations is learned by everyone who grew up in a normal family. That is where, what David Graeber calls 'baseline communism,' is practiced. Within the family, patriarchs or matriarchs may try to lay down the law but, in the end, the principle of 'to each according to their need, from each according to their ability' is the norm, in the family.

Libertarian socialism extends this familial spirit of cooperation beyond the confines of blood relationships to larger social groupings. Siblings are usually friends because they have learned to know each other well. Non-blood related people, working or living together, in free association, with no coercion from without, will usually develop the same kind of fraternal spirit. Individuals who fail to bond with a particular group are free to find another. And freedom must also include the right to remain solitary. But absolute individual isolation is never possible. Everyone must eat[21] and even if a hermit grows his own food, he is still dependent on society to allocate the portion of land he needs to grow his own food—implying property rights and laws enforcing them.

❧

Up to this point, we have outlined a utopia that is so far removed from the present state of affairs that a thousand objections to it can instantly be raised. Some may argue that the proposal would not work because it's not within the bounds of human nature. Others would see existing institutions, corporate and governmental, as so powerful and entrenched that radical alternatives, even if theoretically viable, are impossible to achieve in practice, and therefore worthless.

But this philosophical theory or political philosophy (and where is the distinction?) can only advocate a direction, a progressive direction to be preferred over others. It is not teleological. Not Hegelian. Rather it is emergent.

Is it emerging? yes, or rather, yes, but ...

There are abundant signs that increasing numbers of people are questioning the values of the market society we have become. Many are acting to downsize their rate of consumption in their personal lives, on ethical, health, and/or economic grounds. Co-operative enterprises are growing in number and size. Intentional communities, transition towns, social enterprises, edible landscaping activism, community gardening, and outbreaks of spontaneous citizen protest are becoming more common. The radical impulse in these latter is expressed in banners such as:

CHANGE THE SYSTEM, NOT THE PLANET

The problem is that these healthy green shoots have, so far, barely even begun to displace any of the capitalist global monoculture. It too is growing, in spite of its present difficulties. It will grow because it is structurally incapable of achieving a steady state. In this way, the system resembles an organism. It has a choice of only two directions: life and growth, or death and decay. It has all the power to choose, and it will never choose the latter. Even though it knows it is consuming and destroying the finite resources on which it feeds-or such is one form of conventional wisdom.

To back out of this cul-de-sac we must deconstruct the assumptions that lie buried in the text.

∽

Consider the phrase 'Head of State.' The head is to the body as the chief, leader, president, or king is to the tribe, state or public body. The first assumption is that of a hierarchy, an individual person is a body ruled by a brain/mind. The second assumption is that all levels of society should mirror this authoritarian structure. So, the man dominates his mate, the father rules the family, owners' rule over tenants, employers over employees, and the Pharaoh over every life form in his dominions.

But as every individual knows, just by a cursory self-examination, this first assumption is wrong. Wildly wrong. We are at least as much motivated by our passions as by our reason. If we are honest with ourselves, we will admit that the latter are more often the servant of the former than vice versa. We are, a priori, creatures of feeling, and feelings emerge from the whole body (including its head).

Thinking is largely about constructing narratives that will leave us not feeling guilty about the ways we feel. Above all we want to feel good about ourselves.

Foucault, for example, grew up in a society that regarded homosexual identity as a choice people make, and one defined as abnormal, immoral and criminal. Since he had himself been born with a male body and same-sex urges, he set to work to expose the fallacies in the prevailing mythology. He analyzed the power of professional institutions. These are empowered by society to enforce public acceptance and acquiescence in their 'professional opinions.' As a leading originator of post modernism, he helped to change public perceptions and moved the modern world into a more tolerant and better place.

Post modernism, by exposing all institutional and customary forms of authority to questioning, 'changed the game.' It now becomes possible to question even the most universally established institutions. For example, whether the division of the world into sovereign states is really necessary or desirable. Both the tyranny of the majority, and the attribution of quasi-divine powers to market forces, can now come under critical scrutiny.

The human, like any other animal, resembles a cooperative association of organs more than a brain-ruled monarchy, according to biologists. We should expect a group of organisms to exhibit a similar structure. But so far, ethology has discovered dominance hierarchies everywhere it looks. Anthropology would be hard put to find any instance of a human society devoid of a dominance hierarchy—to some extent.

In pre-literate societies, it was natural for the oldest members to be respected as the best-informed transmitters of the culture. It was wisest to follow their advice in dealing with problems since they were the most likely to have seen similar events before.

∽

Hence, gerontocracy was probably the earliest form of social organization. This would rarely have been oppressive. The elderly maybe wiser but they are inevitably weaker, physically. A patriarch could express his will but could not enforce it without the cooperation of a select group of younger men. This amounted to a system of 'checks and balances.'

Modern society presents us with the opposite condition. Information is ubiquitous and overflowing far beyond the capacity of any one individual to absorb. It is all there on the Internet. Nowadays, an elderly person may have a good memory but nowhere near the capacity of any computer that even a child can easily access.

We have reached a stage in development where the last shred of any justification for dominance hierarchies has been blown away. We no longer need states, armies, drones, ministers, generals, presidents, CEO's, class warfare, money, markets and monocultures.

All we need is love—and I. T.

Because we humans now know there are other conscious non-human beings[22] on this planet, our love is bound to extend to them. We will want to share the land surface with them equitably, recognizing that their natural habitat is different from our artificial one, but also recognizing our common need for uncontaminated water, food, air—and love.

Because of our shared inheritance we will not be surprised to discover that we humans feel attracted to wilderness, and feel a sense of healing when we experience it directly. Conversely, we increasingly feel the same stresses in occupying the modern city as any wild animal would feel, though to a lesser degree.

Seduced by the incredible achievements of our ever-advancing technology, humanity is becoming separated from its roots in the Organic. We are in danger of forgetting the overarching purpose of the Machinic—which is to free people from toil and servitude so that they have more and more time to:

1. Enjoy the joys and beauties of ordinary life in the presence of each other and other life forms;
2. Strive for self-fulfillment in pursuit of objective knowledge (the sciences) and;
3. Strive for self-fulfillment in the creation of objects embodying subjective knowledge (the arts).

But the *application* of science to technologies has served all sorts of purposes other than the overarching one.

The elevation of free *markets* as the guiding principle of economics has not resulted in any significant rise in the proportionate numbers of free *people*. Most people, on the contrary, have found themselves with less and less free time, as the complexities of modern life, themselves the product of advancing technology, have required increasing attention to acquiring the means of access to it.

Organic/machinic is a polarity not a dichotomy. Modern life necessarily involves human participation in both. The point of the distinction is to clarify zones of conflict that are abundant in our world.

It is a fundamental axiom of Organicity that the machinic should always serve the organic and never the other way around.

The following is a simple illustration of this principle:

Consider the case of a five-year-old child of either sex, of any class or culture who lives in a big city. How often is this child free to do what it wants to do, namely, to run out of its home directly, un-supervised, through greenery, to join a bunch of its own age group and to play with them? Rarely. Instead it must usually negotiate with a parent or sibling to go with them, down the lift (possibly), out onto the street and then walk or be driven to the nearest playground. If the streets are busy it will not be quite safe to allow the child to cross them by themselves.

The child is *not* free to do what it wants to do but the people in their cars *are* free to drive anywhere. The city provides continuity for the movement of machines but fragmentation for the movement of pedestrians.

The auto-city is machinic dominated. The organic is to an extent forced to serve the machinic, as a consequence of *its* demands.

We need an organic urbanism or Organi-City.

⁂

The empowerment of collectives small enough to enable self-government and self-employment, by direct democracy, but big enough to contain sufficient expertise to maintain independence, would be good. People would prefer such a life style if given the chance to attain it.

That such a movement would also be a key component of addressing both the ecological and the economic crises will be the subject of a later chapter or two.

To the extent that such a movement radically opposes the status quo, and how to address this fact, will be the subject of another chapter.

Another chapter will attempt to arrive at some principles for evaluating alternative systems using different bio/techno combinations.

Notes

[18] *Adam Smith had warned that Capitalism would fail if it was not tempered with some degree of social conscience.*

[19] *Even the desire for solitude, to be left alone, involves others. Just that we desire to exclude them. Normally this is a temporary wish, followed later by a need for company.*

[20] *The Mondragon Corporation in Spain's Basque country, being a shining exception to the rule.*

[21] *Although it is interesting to note that studies have shown, fasting, counter-intuitively, improves health. So, incidentally, does a vegan diet.*

[22] *The Cambridge Declaration has this year offered definitive scientific proof of this.*

CHAPTER 2

THE ORGANIC/MACHINIC DICHOTOMY

Organicity is an attempt to formulate a coherent meta-philosophy from a set of basic principles taken to be axiomatic:

1. Life (and death) on earth manifests as a series of cycles of interdependence where organisms, atmosphere, soil, sun and wind are in a continuum of dynamic mutual adaptation, in which nothing goes to waste. Normally the system maintains a state of 'fugitive equilibrium.'[23] Abnormal events, such as the impacts of Massive Meteors or Mechanized Man, result in mass extinctions.[24] The earth then resets itself, growing a new stable eco-system out of the few organism's hardy enough to have survived. This takes thousands of years.

2. Human beings evolved on earth from other similar animals who also evolved. All animals have consciousness,[25] feel pain and pleasure, experience love and hate, communicate with their own kind,[26] make decisions,[27] and have 'joie de vivre.'[28] There are examples of some non-human species that have a sense of humor,[29] are curious to learn new things,[30] create and perform works of art[31] and practice complex systems of farming.[32]

3. Such findings bear out Darwin's assertion that humans differ from other animals in degree but not in kind.

When Hobbes saw nature as 'red in tooth and claw,' he was generalizing on the basis of observing one small part of animal behavior. This was inter-specific violence between predator and prey. The cooperative nature of most intra-specific relations had not been noticed or explored in Hobbes's time. He, like Marx, saw humanity's main task to be the control and domination of nature, to free us all from its ugly imperatives.

4. Organisms consist of intimately interconnected organs (themselves likewise composed of cells) that cooperate to form the organism's will to act. The brain is vital to the organism's functioning, but no more so than any of its other organs. Colonies of species-specific organisms are most stable and sustainable to the degree they mimic the cooperative nature of an organism's internal structure. Nature favors fractal formations.

5. Kropotkin was ahead of his time in reporting his own observations of the natural world. He saw that, not only was the practice of mutual aid normative within the specific group but was even observed inter-specifically among the more intelligent animals. In his book, *'Mutual Aid,'* he went further to suggest that *human* institutions based on the cooperative principle had always been associated historically with the most productive and creative periods. He cites the Greek polis and the mediaeval guild system as two examples.

The Organic is easily defined. It is the life of terrestrial organisms, including the human, as they interact with each other and with their environment. Every individual organism is a unique creation but is, at the same time, a mere moment in an infinite web of *connections* extended through space and time. Organisms relate through feeling and affect. It is the domain of Eros.

The Machinic defines that set of human products, relations, and ways of thinking and making, *disconnected* with itself and with the web of life. The Machinic chops up social life, either intentionally or collaterally. Machines and mechanisms are replicable in exact copies, unlike organisms. They operate through the logic of cause and effect. It is the domain of Logos.

The prevailing market based economic system is machinic in some of its effects, and disruptive of the organic. It tends to separate all healthy working age individuals from their familial and communal matrices. Traditionally, extended families and neighborhood communities had constituted mutual support networks and many social goods were accessible in the commons, which has now become largely commercialized. It severs organic connections and replaces them with the cash nexus, over which people have no control whatever. They are atomized, and thus disempowered. The neo-liberal faith that idolizes individual freedom has instead given rise to a new form of addiction, consumerism, in which isolated individuals compete to better themselves over other individuals instead of sharing with others in organic groupings. The byproduct of this personal competition, both within corporations and among consumers, is—huge amounts of waste—hence damage to the environment and resulting climate chaos.

We urgently need to restore the balance between domination, or, let us say, hierarchy—and mutual aid. Violence is ruled out as a means, because violence is itself only the gloved fist of domination. The changes must be peaceful and participatory— whether from the bottom up or from the top down. The turn towards cooperation and direct democracy will first appear in the work place, not in the neighborhoods. Indeed, they are already slowly gaining ground in that arena.

In the long run (if there is a long run), people will come together where they live, to share and enjoy each other's company in the presence of other nature in all its neglected variety and complexity. Only then will the economic system be fully transformed in the direction of sustainability.

The term sustainability is now a commonplace, and is generally understood as something we should strive for. Implicit is the idea that conventional agriculture, for instance, is *not* sustainable. A sustainable form of agriculture would build, not deplete topsoil, maintain, not lower water tables, provide fertilizer from within its own processes, recognize 'pests' as forms of life susceptible to control by other life forms without the use of poisons, and finally would yield good, untainted, vegan food.

Are we advocating a return to pre-industrial methods? No. Machinic is not the same as modern. It is that part of technology that is life negating in effect or in its side effects. It is myopically anthropocentric.

More farsighted technology will be needed to repair the ravages to our global ecosystem brought about by the Machinic. We need to reform our technology to conserve life itself, not just human life. We need to develop an Eco-technology. For example, to reduce waste of water in agriculture, drip irrigation, universalized, might be the eco-tech solution. Modernity is a victim of its own success. The biosphere is a victim of humanity's excess. The notion of progress needs re-definition. Until its benefits are more fairly distributed among the families of humans and other animals, what good is it?

⤟

Consider the archetypical machine, a car. By its means a couple with children can move themselves as a unit, at high speed, to a place of recreation where they can all have fun together, in the presence, often, of other families and wild life, in an arboreal or seaside setting. As such, it is a marvelous thing, serving to strengthen the bonds of family life and facilitating organic connectedness.

On the other hand, the growing infrastructure to support a huge global car culture continues to be a major contributor to environmental disaster and unstoppable heat gain.

Roads kill—in at least three ways. Sealing the land surface kills all the micro-organisms in the soil below the slab, by starving them of air, light and moisture. Every hectare of sealed land reduces the area of productive land, that is the land that feeds plants that feed animals (including the human), by the same degree.

Traffic often kills living organisms trying to cross from one part of their habitat to another, that the road has divided. We correctly call this road kill.

In cities, the sharing of the public space between pedestrian and vehicular traffic leads to accidents, occasionally killing people, their pets and some wildlife. This is ameliorated by establishing speed limits, signage and traffic lights. These trade increased safety for pervasive interruption of the free movement of all citizens, both inside and outside their vehicles.

It is not the machine itself that is necessarily machinic, but all that is entailed in its widespread use. The human uses the car. The car uses the road. The road uses (kills) the micro-organisms in the soil. The worker in the factory uses other machines (made by other workers) to make the car. The factory owner uses the worker, in the same sense that the worker uses a machine, as an object.

Kant's categorical imperative, *'We must not use other human beings as mere means—must not treat them as mere things,'* needs extension to include other animals who are now known to be conscious beings like us.[33] But even before we reach that point there is great need for reform within the modern human community itself. To use human beings to perform endless boring tasks is to treat them as 'mere things.'

Kantian morality is theoretically accepted by most people who nevertheless live in a world where it is everywhere systematically violated. Many are resigned to the status quo, seeing it as an inevitable consequence of modern life with all its proliferating appurtenances.

With its massive investment in the infrastructure of modern life, both physical and institutional, it seems almost impossible to envision, let alone implement, the great 'greening' that must occur if we are to avert climate catastrophe. Climate scientists offer us only a narrow window of a few years to achieve this, globally.

⚖️

Naomi Klein wrote:

> *The real solutions to the climate crisis, are also our best hope of building a much more enlightened economic system—one that closes deep inequalities, strengthens and transforms the public sphere, generates plentiful, dignified work, and radically reins in corporate power.*

The point that Organicity tries to make is that whilst Klein is absolutely right, she places the cart before the horse. Great systemic changes are not going to come about as a result of problem solving, particularly a problem as elusive and esoteric as global heating. Scientists have told us that freak weather patterns will become more frequent as a first sign of impending catastrophe in the future. But ordinary citizens just experience freak weather, and this is only an immediate threat for those who are affected by a particular instance of it. They've 'seen it all before.' They are not going to rise up in anger about changing weather patterns. But they might if unemployment reaches a certain pitch of pain.

Richard Wolff, in his expose of the economic meltdown—brilliantly analysed in the film 'Capitalism Hits the Fan,' points out that boards of directors of a few giant MNC's have great power to resist and subvert any attempt made by governments to regulate them. That is why government regulation has not worked and will not work.

He ends with one existing model of the kind of change needed. It was a case where a bunch of unemployed software engineers in the Silicon Valley of California came together and started a new company in which they themselves comprised, at the same time, the workers, *and* the board of directors. It is a cooperative, not headless, but multi-headed organism, with no hierarchy. It is organic in structure, not machinic.

Another example of the same kind of collective is the Star & Shadow Cinema in Newcastle,UK.

Notes

23   *Kropotkin's term.*
24   *We humans are causing the sixth mass extinction since the beginning of life on earth.*
25   *The Cambridge Declaration.*
26   *Using body language and/or 'calls'.*
27   *Fight or flight?/Go left or right?*
28   *Observe any pet dog taken out for a walk.*
29   *Crows have been observed pecking a sheep on one side and quickly hopping over to its other side as it turns to investigate.*
30   *Curiosity never killed the cat. On the contrary, combined with its equally strong sense of caution, it helped it survive.*
31   *Bower birds, two other Australian species of bird, and at least one species of male fish does the same on the sea floor. (Deleuze pp 184)*
32   *Leaf cutter ants*
33   *See, The Cambridge Declaration.*

CHAPTER 3

TO BE OR NOT TO BE

Many have concluded that there is no hope for the human species. The problems of overgrowth of population, consumption, and carbon emissions, seem too huge and inexorable to stop, or even to slow down.

And even if some unimaginable revolutionary upheaval led to the adoption of a steady state economic system to replace the existing globalized capitalist growth engine, this would still fall short of sustainability, since we are told by ecologists that the world is already exploiting the terrestrial bio-capacity at a rate 1.5 times that at which it can be renewed.

The distribution of the goods derived from these resources, are now lopsided. One fifth of the global population are hungry while another fifth are so over-fed that many are suffering the health consequences related to obesity.

It is not just a question of the fair distribution of goods, though that is urgently needed. The total product must be reduced to fit within finite earthly limits.

The 'developed' world has not come to terms with the fact that it is truly 'over-developed.' Not only are we, the over-developed, consuming seven slices of the pie and leaving one slice for the under-developed, but we have yet to face the fact that the *pie itself must be made smaller.*

It must so happen if we wish our progeny to live in a world something like the one we still do enjoy living in.

The Ontology of Organicity

Organicity re-prioritizes human values by shifting human perspective away from the anthropocentric towards the biocentric. Just as the Copernican revolution displaced our earth from centrality in the solar system, so organicity displaces one species, the human, from centrality in the earthly biosphere.

Organicity affirms the primacy of earthly life and the well-being of the global eco-system. It recognizes the essential continuity and affinity between the human and other conscious beings. We call this the Organic

Organi-City (in its other spelling) recognizes the existence and indispensability of the artificial world built up around the human species, especially since the Industrial Revolution. This world has expanded our consciousness in many directions. It has lengthened our lives and lifted the burden of meaningless toil for many of us. In the process, it has distracted us from protecting those goods and beauties which we, as terrestrials, hold most dear. Inadvertently, we are undermining the very conditions of our survival as social animals.

Classical philosophy establishes the I, as subject (and the thou, as object?). Organicity proposes the We and the It. 'We' includes all living organisms including the human. 'It' constitutes all machines, all things machine made, and all institutions exemplifying the User/Used relationship, regardless of whether either side happens to be subject or object. We call this whole assemblage the 'Machinic.'[34]

Organicity is a philosophy of harmonizing the Organic and the Machinic. Each ought to be given its own space and tempo. Both are necessary sides of the human but up to now they have invaded each other's space to the detriment of the functioning of each.

The Epistemology of Organicity

Doubt grows with knowledge, Goethe said.

Recent developments in science have certainly confirmed his insight. In cosmology, we are now led to believe that most of the universe consists of dark energy and dark matter. In other words, we have found out so much about the cosmos that we now realize, most of it is composed of something about which we know nothing.

General relativity tells us that gravity is really the rolling around of bodies in the curvature of space/time. But it doesn't feel like that.

Quantum electrodynamics would have us accept that the particles from which all matter is constructed do not exist except when observed. The rest of the time they are waves. We also find that quanta can move backwards in time and also force us to accept the principle of non-locality. When quantum physicists talk about their experiments, they often resort to anthropomorphisms to explain the behavior of particles that seem to know about alternative path B, even when they decide to follow path A. They not only come into existence when observed, but know in advance when they are going to be observed.

Common sense tells us that things are what they seem. Modern science continually assures is that this is not so.

Evolution has supplied us with just sufficient sensory organs to flourish in relation to our natural environment. But we have evolved a brain that can devise extensions to our given senses, and these have discovered a universe that literally doesn't make sense.

❦

Why is it that the human mind baulks at duality? Philosophers have struggled for eons to grapple with the issue that we simply cannot accept the mind/body duality.

But nature is awash with dualities: male/female, wave/particle, alive/dead, mind/body, positive/negative polarity, etc. It looks as if the nature of nature is to be dual. Perhaps the fundamental one is that of attraction/repulsion—seemingly present even in chemicals.

In the oscillation of the moving together and the recoil, energy and life is generated—and not just in the sexual sense.

Scientists dream of the concept of a 'unified field theory.' Why not accept that there are multiple fields, all pervading the universe (since they are non-material they can coexist in the same space/time)?

There are two known fields, gravitational and electro-magnetic.

Sheldrake hypothesizes a third field, which he calls the morphic field. This does not solve the mind/body problem but it shifts it into territory analogous with QED. To the extent that we are forced to accept that particles move as a wave and arrive as a particle, we should also be prepared to accept an electrical impulse that pulses through neurons and synapses and arrives at a thought. But the thought 'exists' in an immaterial sense—in the morphic field.

⸕

Goethe posited a third force. Deeply imprinted in the nature of things are attraction/repulsion. The third force he called intensification.

Biologists have built on Darwin's revolutionary insights.

The theory of natural selection, genetics, and chance mutations explain how life forms came into being. But some biologists believe these concepts are necessary but not sufficient.

Perhaps 'intensification' is the missing ingredient. After all, genetic mutations are blind forces and it becomes hard to believe conscious beings have no influence on their own growth. We baulk, and I think rightly, at accepting genetic determinism as the be all and end all. Conscious beings, in part, become what they want to become. Without the acknowledgement of free will we would have no way of judging our conduct. There could be no Ethics.

The Ethics of Organicity

Human and other conscious beings are subjects. They should never be treated as objects. This is the first principle of Organicity.

John Stuart Mill asserted that society should aim at 'the greatest happiness of the greatest number (of sentient beings).' He proposed that people should be allowed to do what they like so long as they do not harm others.[35] In the end he veered more and more to the left and towards what amounted to the replacement of capitalism by libertarian socialism.

Organicity builds on Mill and, starting where he left off, updates his theory to conform to contemporary conditions and changing values in the light of developments in psychology, natural history, political science and ecology. The 'greatest number' must include, particularly, all conscious beings, and also future generations, not just the present population.

⤬

The current wage system paradigm, almost universally accepted, is that an employee voluntarily enters into a contract with an employer. He/she is then required to spend forty hours a week under the command of the employer for an agreed wage.

In other words, the employer buys the right to *use* the employee for any legal purpose during the stipulated hours. The employer owns the employee, during working hours, just as he/she owns the product, permanently, that the employees create.

But ownership and use of a human being violates the first principle. Employees are being treated as objects. Happiness does not result from obeying someone else's commands but from fulfilling our own desires. While we are not free, we cannot even focus on our desires, except for the single desire that the clock should strike 5 pm.

But supposing I am *self*-employed—not as an individual, but as part of a collective, a group that has assembled with a common interest in making something?

The collective discusses how best to make the product, what hours should be worked, who does what, and for how much reward, and how the proceeds of the sale of the product should be allocated. If management is required, the manager is elected by the collective from one of their own group. He/she will be subject to instant recall, should the collective decide performance has been inadequate.

This is anarcho-syndicalism. There is no question that workers would be happier if it was adopted. It would seem that real progress now demands it for the following reason. At the moment, the steady increase in automation has had the effect, under capitalism, of increasing unemployment.

Under anarcho-syndicalism, automation would be welcomed, not feared. Replacing humans with robots would enable the collective to reduce working hours, so that more people might choose to participate in the more mentally challenging jobs, or educate themselves for some new branch of the enterprise. Factory benches easily convert to classroom desks as has been frequently found whenever workers gain control.

Co-operatives are a good first step towards anarcho-syndicalism and their numbers are growing but it is doubtful that they are growing at the *expense* of private capital. Unfortunately, overall growth is the last thing the world needs.

⚭

What about the 'other conscious beings' included in the first principle?

42

Well people don't treat their pets as objects. On the contrary, most pet owners regard their pets as members of their families.

Farm animals are something else. On small family farms they may be treated somewhat like friends—at least up until the day they are butchered.

Factory farming is a complete horror show. If it had been designed to demonstrate the negative proposition, 'the greatest *un*happiness of the greatest number,' it could not have been bettered.

Ethical consumers are coming to understand that meat eating is bad, and we should all try to move in the direction of a vegan diet. If animals are subjects, then the injunction, 'thou shalt not kill,' applies to them. A vegan diet has been proven to be healthier than an omnivorous one. It has been calculated that the meat industry, as a whole, produces as much greenhouse gas as all the cars on the road. Lastly, growing animal feed requires at least ten times the land area needed for growing the equivalent food value. One hectare of cropland feeds ten vegetarians or one carnivore. It cannot do both.

It may be argued that ovo/lacto vegetarians are not animal killers. But per first principles, they still are *using* animals. Strictly speaking, therefore, they are treating subjects as objects. Unless they can prove that in particular cases, this egg was freely given by a happy hen, or, this cheese made from the milk of a happy cow, who eagerly returned from a lush green meadow to the barn and enjoyed being milked.

Last time I checked at Morrison's. I saw no such testaments printed on these products and I am not sure I would believe it if I did see them.

What should our attitude be to wild animals, on land, in sea, and in the air?

We should just let them be and not encroach on their space and drive them to extinction as we are now doing.

There is some mutual curiosity between wild animals and cultivated ones like ourselves. There is no harm in pursuing this if it is done with respect. Animals can communicate non-verbally with each other, and with us, and we can learn much from studying their behavior, which is sometimes more exemplary than our own.

❦

Happiness cannot be legislated nor can it be 'pursued,' the language of the US Constitution notwithstanding. Happiness is the absence of repression. The exercise of freedom results in happiness. But we can deceive ourselves. When we think we are free, we may not be. We cannot help but be constrained by the values, norms, and rules with which we were unconsciously indoctrinated by our parents during early childhood. Typically, the ghosts of our parents sit on our shoulders and, every impulse we have, they whisper in our ears: 'That's wrong. Don't do that' or, more rarely, 'That's right. Do as much of that as you can.'

Freud defined our deepest urges as the Id. He followed the classical tradition of devaluing these primal urges and asserting that they must be controlled, either by submitting to the authority of the Superego or by sublimation into a socially acceptable substitute form. He explored this regrettable necessity in '*Civilization and its Discontents.*'

Wilhelm Reich, Freud's assistant, disagreed with the master in this respect. He challenged the notion that the Id must be repressed. The infant's natural urge to seek out its mother's breast and to suck on its nipple was a benign thing. It did no harm to its mother. On the contrary. This urge was basically sexual and was the prototype of adult sexuality, which also, in a natural loving way, gives and takes pleasure in equal measure.

For Reich, the negative, aggressive urges of the Id were a secondary formation *resulting from the repression* of its primary healthy expression. The acculturation process inevitably corrupts the human animal through the enforcement of its rules, first through the mother, then through the schools, and finally through its internalized absorption of these in a structure of unconsciously mandated inhibitions. This makes us all angry. The anger is then also repressed by our imperious Super-ego.

Society should stop trying to prevent people behaving badly and concentrate on unlocking the goodness that is innate in all of us animals.

A young couple decided to put Reich's ideas into practice and to raise a family as freely as possible. After their children had grown up, Paul and Jean Ritter wrote a book describing their experience. It included frank commentaries by the children and is entitled '*Free Family and Feedback.*' Copies of this book are now rare—and priced accordingly. The children, now middle-aged men and women, are pursuing normal careers in Western Australia. One of them is continuing Paul's work with the institution he founded, called Educreation.

To say that Paul and Jean's experiment was successful doesn't signify much. After all, even shamanism 'works'—in curing diseases and so on. But it does prove that for the normal healthy infant and the child that it becomes, we have nothing to fear from 'letting nature take its course.' And surely that is the right thing to do wherever society permits it. And that society is best which permits it most.

Organicity searches for a natural morality that must have evolved along with life itself.

Civilization's progress up to now could be interpreted as a flight from the animalistic and an elaboration of the myth of human exclusivity. We are now brought down to earth by the realization that, by so doing, we have tried to exclude the most fundamental and authentic part of ourselves. One consequence is the climate crisis. Another is ecocide.

We must change. Climate scientists have been unanimous in showing that 'business as usual' projected to the end of this century would land our offspring in purgatory. We will change. How? Catastrophically, or in an orderly series of steps that cause the least pain to the greatest number?

Bernie Sanders and Charles Fadel, in the current RSA Journal, postulate three 'waves' of modernity. First, was the industrial revolution, second, the factory system of mass production and third, the computerized automation of same. The authors anticipate the beginnings of a 'fourth wave,' now in its early stages, in the local design and fabrication of parts and products using desktop and small computer-controlled equipment.' Such miniaturization of technology bodes well for the necessary re-localization of industry in reaction to its current insane riot of market driven trans-oceanic trading.

However, the frequently cited 'ages' were not successive but cumulative. Human life is just as dependent on agriculture as it ever was, just as dependent on industry as it has been for the last 200 years, and is now only a 'service economy' for a small privileged population.

What has happened is a geographic separation of these three functions accompanied by an exaggerated class distinction that goes in the opposite direction than that which the promise of mass production of cheap goods might have led us to hope for. If a contemporary stone age tribesman from Madagascar met a Wall Street Hedge Fund manager, they would have nothing to say to each other, even if they spoke the same language. Each would feel far more connected with their own pets.

Perchance to Dream

What hope is there? There are three grounds for it.

A. The rapidly rising anger of Gaia. This cannot be hidden or silenced.
B. The Internet's broadcast of the fact that the Emperor has no clothes (or morals). On a level playing field, the truth will triumph over false propaganda.
C. The burgeoning anger of the 99.99%

These three energizers are already in play. Within a very few years they may precipitate major social upheavals, followed by a series of global general strikes. This would certainly result in major changes, which will be positive, provided it proceeds on sound theoretical principles.

Organicity's first principle, that persons should be respected as persons and never used as objects, give rise to several other basic principles appropriate to the new steady state economy/life style:

1. Adoption of cooperation as the default mode of relating, versus competition.
2. Decentralization of power, wealth, and productive capacity from multi-national corporations to local communities.
3. Local communities to be organized as participatory democracies.
4. Re-localization.
5. Recognition that global resources must be allocated fairly by whatever means. No country's population should be left to starve because of desertification caused by more technologically advanced countries who have caused it.
6. The present population of bio-regions should develop participatory plans for achieving a balance between the projected population and the bio-capacity of the region. Big cities together with surrounding agricultural land needed to support their projected populations should be considered bio-regions.
7. These plans should aim at maximum autonomy. That is, as far as reasonably possible, all goods and services should be produced and consumed within the region. However, the principle of sharing adopted by individuals in a community should also prevail between communities and countries. All on the basis of 'From

each according to their ability, to each according to their need.'

8. People should be encouraged to choose the democratic option of adopting Anarcho-syndicalism to replace capitalism within the region.

9. Direct democracy is favored over representative but the latter is favored over any other form of governance.

10. Participatory planning by communities networked into country-wide and ultimately global plans, to replace market forces as a means of allocating resources and products.

11. The consideration of rationing as means to fairly distribute the process of balancing resources with the planned populations of organisms per region. This may need to include rationing of the right to bear children, which could be .5 pp—with the associated right to buy and/or sell another individual's permit allocation.

12. Manufacturing to be re-conceived as a closed loop system with ever diminishing proportions of wasted material and resource extraction.

Notes

[34] *For example, in a typical factory, the managers are subjects but the employees are treated as objects, just like machines. Such a factory is part of the Machinic. On the other hand, a worker owned, operated and managed factory would be part of the Organic.*

[35] *JSM made an exception for those 'incapable of self-government' which included children and implicitly, other animals.*

CHAPTER 4

PARTICIPATORY DEMOCRACY

Mass produced objects are not creations. They are reproductions. Humans can create other humans. That is procreation, not reproduction. Humans can also create works of art. And so, incidentally, can certain animal species.[36] These are also always unique, and this is what distinguishes them from mechanically reproduced artifacts, which are of a different category.

But is not the implication here, that humans are themselves 'unique.' in the sense of being the only animal that makes machines, which are not found anywhere in nature other than in the presence of the humans who produce and use them?

It would be foolish to deny our differences from other animals, which are evident wherever we look around us at the artificial world we have created for ourselves. But this is not something of which we should be proud. It is the source of our problems, our ecological dilemma, our caesura from the biosphere.

But humans are still animals and, like all such, tied to the same branching growth of earthly life, breathing the same air, enjoying the same land, and chained to the same food sources. And every other species exhibits their own differences too.

It was Descartes's Enlightenment/Humanism that filled us with hubris and led us astray into the wasteland of modernity.

The Enlightenment blew away the cobwebs of mysticism and brought us to a healthy respect for things whose existence could be proved. However, in the process, at least one baby was thrown out with the bathwater.

Civilization gained an immeasurably improved tool for the acquisition of true facts; the scientific method.

At the same time, what was lost were two important attributes of the former Christian heritage, our sense of community, and our sense of attunement to natural surroundings.

The Church, for all its failings, had nurtured one article of faith that was subconsciously, but deeply, believed. This was the sense that since God had created the world, then Creation must be, ultimately, good.

Rousseau's attack on the Enlightenment was, in part, a restoration of this core value from the age that preceded it. He asserted that man is naturally good.

His celebration of naturalism, that is the understanding of humans in terms continuous with the sciences of extra human nature, prepared the ground for Darwin's tremendous conclusion that the human animal differs from other animals in degree but not in kind.

Charles Taylor, in his book, '*The Sources of the Self,*' frames modernity as a struggle between Enlightenment and Romanticism. His suggestion is that ecological problems arise when the former dominates society at the expense of the expression of the latter.

Enlightenment pits reason, disengaged freedom, equality and universality against Romanticism's nature, fulfillment, expressive integrity, intimacy and particularity.

E sets instrumental reason to work on an objectified universe. It proposes technological solutions to ecological problems. Romanticism proposes ecological solutions to technologically induced problems.

༄

The right wing says 'privatize everything.' The old left wing used to say 'nationalize everything.' But nobody says 'communalize everything.'

Nevertheless, until the latter demand emerges, and starts to gain traction, there will be no hope for saving the world from 'financial catastrophe, the jobs crisis and environmental destruction.'

But this is an exaggeration. To begin with, there *are* probably a few communitarian socialists still around, surviving apostles of Eric Fromm, who *are* saying 'communalize everything,' but who would listen to their small voices in this day and age?

Then, nobody is so extreme as to really believe you can classify ownership exclusively in any one of these three baskets. You need all three. In fact, you need a fourth, a supranational authority, the UN.

What has gone horribly wrong is that at the moment the vast preponderance of wealth and power has gone to the tiny elite that make up the boards of directors of the giant multi-national corporations. There is only one other repository of power and that is the state. But the state has largely become the hand maiden of the Plutonomy. The elite 1% has become so rich that it no longer needs the other 99%. They are maintaining their wealth by developing an exclusive market catering in luxury goods.

Treating the environment, the people, and the commons, as an externality, only becomes a problem for them when they find, for example, their yachts are now too long to dock in most existing marinas.

> *It is too early to forecast whether banks or governments will emerge victorious from today's crisis. As economies polarize between debtors and creditors, planning is shifting out of public hands into those of bankers. The easiest way for them to keep this power is to block a true central bank or strong public sector from interfering with their monopoly of credit creation. The counter is for central banks and governments to act as they were intended to, by providing a public option for credit creation.* – Michael Hudson

Rousseau – *true freedom is found only in austerity*

Toqueville – *freedom ... offers other objectives than that of getting rich.*

Jefferson – *The mass of mankind has not been born with saddles on their backs, nor a favored few booted and spurred, ready to ride them legitimately, by the grace of God.*

Marx – *capitalist society generates unequal relations of power which make a mockery of the political equality which genuine self-rule pre-supposes.*

Neighbourhood Associations

It should be emphasized that the suggestions that follow are the author's idea of what people, left to themselves, might choose to do, if given the chance.

What they *will* do is for them to decide. The over-riding principle is people power. We have corporate power and popular consent. We need the opposite. But let us sketch a hypothetical possibility.

First the neighborhood must define its territory. The boundaries could be defined by the postal code map, the territory defined by the bus routes, or existing local government maps. It probably needs to contain a preponderance of housing over other uses, and the more diverse it is in terms of income levels, demographics, and work skills the better. The boundaries could be arbitrary but must be determined before the social organization can be set up.

Step One is to locate a building near the center of the territory that contains a single large space unobstructed by columns. This could be adapted from a disused Victorian warehouse, for example, or a disused church. If possible, it should adjoin a public space that could be made traffic free in front of the general assembly building. If no suitable building exists a marquee could be rented or bought and set up temporarily.

Step Two is to invite everyone living and working in the NA to a meeting in the GAB to explain the system of direct democracy and self-government that will be instituted. It will be stressed that all power within the NA lies with the people living and working there. All decisions must be ratified by vote of those assembled at regular weekly meetings in the GAB. They will elect an executive committee, which will only have power to carry out the policies proposed by the assembly. It will have no authority to act outside those declarations of intent.

Step Three will be to explore the options for social change to bring about the betterment of all, through the elimination of waste and through sharing of communal facilities formerly privately owned.

Step Four will be to recognize that the goal of the association is to own everything within its territory. In particular it owns all the land. Therefore, those who own their own homes within the territory will be required to pay a nominal rent for the leasehold of the land on which their property is built.

Notes

36 *Deleuze 'What is Philosophy?' p.184.*

CHAPTER 5

THE THREE EXISTENTIAL CRISES

*Nuclear, ecological, chemical, economic—our arsenal of
Death by Stupidity is impressive for a species as smart as
Homo sapiens.*

Jeanette Winterson, The New York Times,
September 17, 2009

Mutual aid is the predominant fact of nature.

Petr. Kropotkin 'Ethics'(ch.1)1924

The second quotation is the conclusion of a life-long study by
a scientist of nature, following in the footsteps of Darwin. The
first quotation exposes the tragic misapplication of Darwin
to the global economy by the 'Darwinists,' peddling, the false
god—'survival of the fittest.'

To base an economy on the principle of 'survival of the fittest'
is completely irrational, in fact, totally mad. This is because the
phrase carries with it the notion that the less fit *do not* survive. In
other words, we are basing the economy on the idea that the fittest
KILL the less fit. Building into the system whereby things are
produced and distributed for the benefit of all, the principle that

this is best pursued with murderous intent is not only nonsense, but in a real (Kropotkinite) sense *un*natural.

Some will protest that evolution really is driven by a struggle for survival in which the strongest win out. Neither Darwin nor Kropotkin ever denied this but what Darwin was mainly referring to was *reproductive* fitness. And all Kropotkin was adding was that though competition, lethal violence, and individual ego assertion is widespread in nature, it is not *predominant*.

Reproductive fitness refers to those individuals who are the most sexually attractive and this translates to competition to see who can be the most charming. It tends to favour those who are the most cooperative, those who practice mutual aid, those who are 'good' individuals, not murderers or rapists.

This is why violently aggressive and anti-social individuals are not commonly encountered in organic societies (animal and pre-industrial human), even among non-social animals such as cats, owls or gorillas.

Even though male lions have a bad habit of killing the offspring of their new mate's previous lover, there is abundant evidence that tigresses, for example, will sometimes suckle and take care of the young of their prey rather than eating them. The maternal instinct is here shown to be far stronger than the predatory, even operating as it does, across inter species boundaries.

What Hobbes saw when he invoked the phrase 'nature, red in tooth and claw,' was just one side of nature. When we see, for example, a blue jay energetically pecking the last breath out of a sparrow, with repeated blows to the back, head and eyes, for no apparent reason other than that it enjoys murdering 'the (helpless) other,' we are shocked and horrified. We tend to feel 'if this is 'nature,' let's have no part of it—we humans are better than that.'

We tend to forget that the practice of torture, which we humans continue to perform, where the victim is deliberately kept *alive* so that its agony can be prolonged indefinitely, is a far crueler act than the blue jays. We also fail to remember that our deep-seated repugnance of violence directed *at our own kind*, is a direct inheritance from our natural antecedents, as Darwin and Kropotkin make so clear.

Unless we are theists, which few of us in the west any longer are, we must accept that our ethical judgments have a natural origin. Cooperation and competition both operate at all stages in the evolution of life on earth. So presumably, love and tenderness can co-exist with violent hatred in the same subject—for different objects, or even the same object, at different times, in different moods.

All people have the right to participate in all discussions and decisions affecting their individual lives, directly, and not through representatives.

No adult human individual ever has a right to command another adult human individual to obey his/her order(s).

It is always wrong for any human being to kill any other conscious being except in defense against a clear threat to his/her own life.

All conscious beings have the same right to life as human beings.

The Ecological Crisis

Unprecedented and damaging weather events all over the world are at last convincing the general public that what climate scientists have been warning about is unfortunately true.

Destabilization of the weather is only the least part of the problem brought on by consumerism and the winner-take-all economic system that feeds it.

What is damaging to the eco-system in the way of life we have developed in most of the northern hemisphere, breaks into three parts: quantitative, qualitative and spiritual.

The quantitative aspect is best understood through the 'footprint theory' (Wackernagel). The quantity of earth's renewable resources that are required to support any individual leading a certain way of life can be measured and expressed as the land area required to deliver it. The same measure can be applied to cities, regions, nations and finally the whole globe.

For any country, the total footprint of its population can be compared with its productive land area. Each country will fall either above or below its bio-capacity. The developed world, which rightly should be called the over-developed world, exists mostly in the northern hemisphere. The developing world (formerly known as the third world) should be called the under-developed world. It occupies most of the southern hemisphere.

Globally, it has been revealed that the human population as of this century, is using Earth's renewable resources at a rate 1.5 times its bio-capacity.

Obviously, this is unsustainable and means that future generations in the over-developed countries will need to lower their standards of living substantially until they recover equilibrium with the planet's natural cycles. The only alternative would be a drastic reduction in the human population.

The quantitative analysis begs questions. *Can* the human population be reduced in numbers, humanely? Can more efficient technologies be developed to enable us to do more with less? Can we, in the over-developed world, *choose* to live more simply, with fewer luxuries?

We trust that, not only can these questions be answered in the affirmative, but that doing so will lead to an increase, not a decrease in overall well-being.

Considering now the qualitative aspect, it is not just that capitalism converts resources into products too much and too fast, but also the *kind* of products that it sees fit to produce. Products that cause carbon emissions, either in their use or during their manufacturing stage, cause damage to the eco-system, to the extent that the emissions exceed the earth's capacity to absorb them.

The best example of this qualitative misfit is the energy source on which all other industries depend: fossil fuels.

No civilization utterly dependent on below ground extraction of relatively rare materials can hope to last very long. Such materials are inevitably exploited at a far faster rate than their natural replacement. But this is not the main problem. That is the accumulation of CO2 and other greenhouse gases in the atmosphere that the burning of fossil fuels entails.

The two quotations that follow encapsulate the problem:

> *If humanity wishes to preserve a planet similar to that on which civilization developed and to which life on Earth is adapted, paleo-climate evidence and ongoing climate change suggest that CO_2 will need to be reduced from its current 385 ppm to at most 350 ppm. – James Hansen.*

> *The International Energy Agency also warned that the world may not be able to limit temperature rise if new international climate action is not taken by 2017 as so many fossil fuel power plants and factories are being built. … A new global climate pact forcing the world's biggest polluters, including the United States and China, to curb emissions will only be agreed on by 2015—to enter into force by 2020—seen by many as too late to limit climate damage. – Club of Rome*

But the insights of deep ecology (Arne Naess) are perhaps the only way in which the human spirit will be brought back to an appreciation and love for its earthly origin.

The central tenet of deep ecology is that other animals and life forms have intrinsic value. Life has a right to life. We accept that *we* have a right to life. We now see, through our ecological misdeeds, that we should have adopted the larger principle at the start of the industrial revolution.

No normal person hates animals, although as with any other species, our right to life includes the right to defend ourselves against attack by another. This was as true when we faced saber toothed tigers as it is today with bacteria and viruses.

We are not threatening the extinction of some of the most rare, complex, intelligent and beautiful creatures on earth because we feel threatened by them, but because they 'get in the way' of the ordinary operation of the huge heartless machines that cater to what we have been led to believe are our needs.

Trawlers carelessly scrape the bottom of the oceans, or net and kill porpoises, while gathering their marketable catch. Indonesian palm oil interests bulldoze forest cover where the last few remaining orangutans struggle to survive. The Amazon, the biggest and most important carbon sink on the planet is encroached on daily by agri-business, relentlessly expanding their land area for soybean production to feed the lucrative meat industry. Sharks are dying in agony on the ocean floor, having had their fins removed for soup, a supposed aphrodisiac.

Capitalism has largely managed to hide from the consumer, the means by which it produces what the consumer wants. Thus, it has fostered the illusion that human nature is fundamentally different from nature itself. Big business operates best in big cities, where goods arrive in packages, far from the machines and people who did the packaging, and even further from the natural origin of the goods themselves.

The Economic Crisis

One of the shibboleths of neo-liberalism, on which the current global economic system is based, is that free markets create wealth at the top but that it will 'trickle down.' It did contain an element of truth, at least during the first twenty years following WW2.

During that period, in the advanced industrial economies, the wages of workers kept pace with their rising levels of productivity. Some wealth did indeed 'trickle down.' Not since.

Since the 1970's, wages have stagnated while productivity has continued to rise (Hudson). The increased profits have enriched mainly the financial services industry.

Meanwhile, manufacturing has been largely 'outsourced' to emerging economies—mainly China but also other countries in south east Asia and India.

The 'hollowing out' of the economies of the western democracies combined with reckless gambling by owners of capital, has now resulted in increasing hardship, unemployment, and rising civil unrest, especially in USA and the southern tier of European states—the PIGS (Portugal, Ireland, Greece and Spain).

There is now an economic crisis on top of, and distinct from, the ecological crisis. But both crises have the same cause. Capitalism does one thing extremely well. It accumulates more and more capital in the hands of fewer and fewer people, in an endless cycle of profiteering.

The climate, earth ecology, wild life and increasingly large numbers of the human global population are external to this process, and therefore not taken into consideration by corporate planners. As a consequence:

> *Europe's Mediterranean rim trembled on Wednesday as violent clashes broke out following the largest coordinated multinational strike in Europe ever. In the hope to stave off decades of austerity, precarity and unemployment, European labor unions united for the first time since the start of the European debt crisis to organize strikes and protests in a total of 23 EU member states, with millions of workers walking off their jobs and marching on parliament buildings across the continent. Bloody street battles ensued across Spain, Portugal and Italy ... And so Southern Europe continues to tremble on its very foundations. As smoke rises from the streets of Madrid, Lisbon,*

> *Rome and Athens, one thing is becoming ever more clearer: the question is no longer if but when the social explosion will hit. The outrage is building up, and with unemployment rising, austerity deepening, and a generation of Europeans increasingly disillusioned by state intransigence and outraged by police violence, such an outburst of popular rebellion seems ever more inevitable. All it will take is a spark. – Jerome E. Roos 15/11/12*

The fact that this strike action barely received a mention in the mainstream media is a measure of how far the authorities feel threatened. They do not want to fan the flames of smoldering discontent by drawing attention to it.

The Crisis of Neoliberalism

The notion that markets left to run free of all government regulation will lead to the best of all possible worlds has certainly been proved false. But does this imply that greater state control of the economic system would increase prosperity and equality? No.

The present situation varies from country to country but, in general, whilst national governments, in theory, have authority over their industries, including their banks, in practice, multinational corporations have such enormous financial resources they can and do dictate to national leaders, not the other way around.

Hence, we heard recently, of banks that were 'too big to fail.' The conclusion was, since they *were* failing, they must be 'bailed out' by government. Who is in charge here? Certainly not the common people.

Even in nominal democracies, such as the USA, the mainstream media is to such an extent owned by the corporations themselves, that any serious challenge to their power is all but inconceivable through the electoral system. This is because candidates for office, regardless of their politics, cannot hope to have their message heard without massive TV exposure, and this is very expensive. The elite will not provide the necessary funding of this for anyone they don't like.

If systemic change is to come about it will need to come through the direct action of the people themselves. The Occupy Wall Street movement is a significant first step in this direction. It is predominantly a middle-class protest outraged at the huge and ever widening gap between the wealth and income of the '1%' and the '99%.'

The recent general strike across the EU, was led by the unions. As such, it was an action by pre-existing organizations coordinating their plans across national boundaries. This perhaps was the second step. Stay tuned.

But confrontation by activists representing the majority of ordinary people against 'the powers that be' does not, in itself, change the world. It is more of a symptom than a solution, although important in bringing the issue of inequality back into the public discourse (Chomsky).

As environmental designers we are concerned with the way socio/economic systems are embodied in their physical manifestations, especially in the big cities where an ever-increasing percentage of the global population is destined to live.

Let us first consider the history of the city over recent centuries in the belief that, understanding where we have come from, what we have gained and lost, will enable us to make plausible suggestions for improving the lot of the average citizen, in the near future.

❧

We are running out of time. We know that our present way of life endangers the future viability of all life on earth. We know how to eliminate that danger—by outlawing the extraction of fossil fuels.

But our globalized economic system, which has infiltrated every aspect of our lives, a system now seen to be fatally flawed, seems too big to transform, at least not in the narrow window of time deemed necessary by scientists.

How do people respond to this crisis? One can identify ten ways which break down into five pairs, for in some ways they represent mirrored approaches:

1. Denial
2. Fatalistic acceptance
3. Rejection of modern technology—back to pre-industrial ways
4. Faith in modern technology—leading us to another planet
5. Faith in God
6. Voluntary asceticism (by individuals)
7. Forming intentional communities and organizing at neighborhood scale
8. Forming work cooperatives and practicing direct democracy
9. Faith in beneficent power of natural evolution
10. Honoring and cherishing mother earth before all things

CHAPTER 6

ORGANI-_CITY_:
(THE MATRIPOLE)

Figure 1 is one of the boards from the Integrated Habitats Design Competition of 2010 which we, the author and Dr Paul Jones of Northumbria University Architecture Department, were awarded Runner Up status. The board is entirely the work of Paul and the design mostly mine, based on my Matripolis idea from my first book: '_The End of the Street._' Matripolis = OrganiCITY.

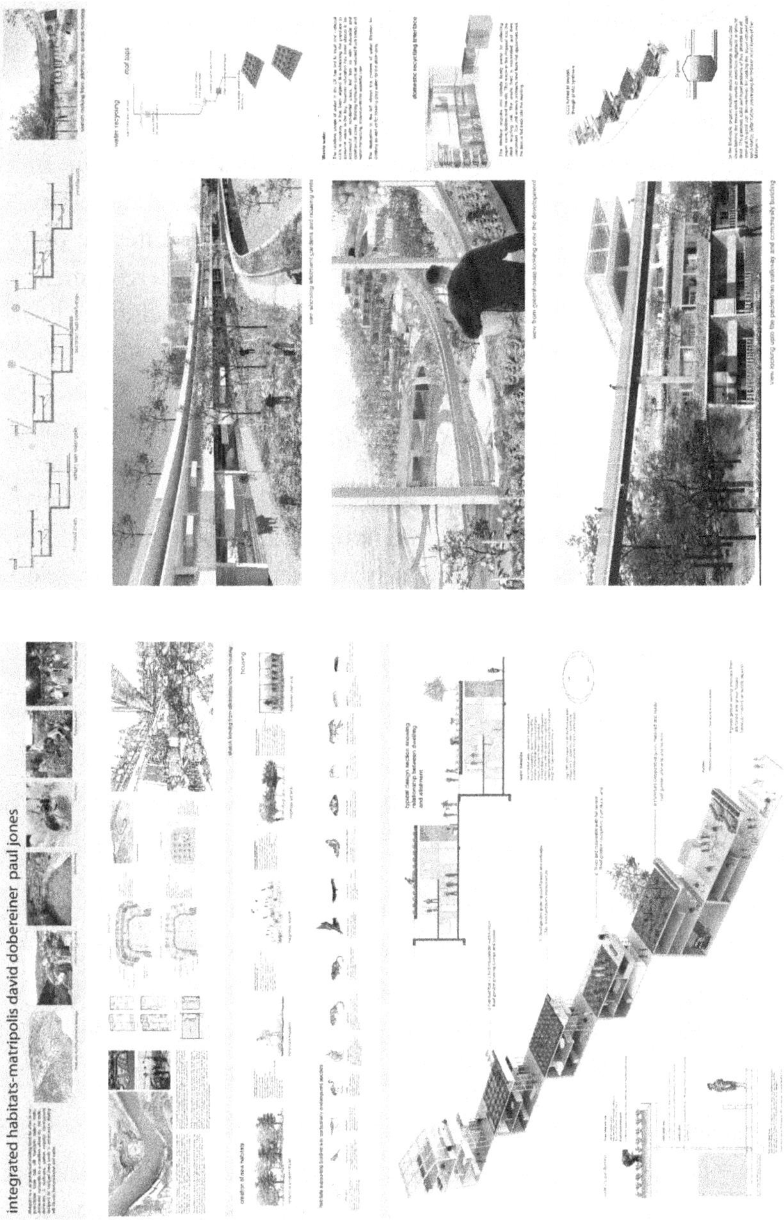

Figure 1

Integrated Habitat

The word 'habitation' applies to the human's home but the sense of 'home' is also strongly expressed in the word 'habitat' as we apply it to all other animals. This separate vocabulary we insist on, in order to distance ourselves from all other species (as if humanity had evolved on some other planet) is then made manifest in our built environment. So typically, we have urban development carpeting the earth with hard material, repellent to all other life forms—surrounded by what we call the 'environment' where biodiversity reigns.

Yet we humans love to immerse ourselves in the wilderness. We leap at any chance we have to wander among trees, listen to bird song, witness squirrel antics, and marvel at the striking design of butterfly wings. But we have been programmed to treat such leisure activity as completely separate from our domestic space.

We can imagine one cabin in the woods, like Thoreau's. But how could a whole neighborhood of 500 people be planned so that every single person could step directly from their front door into a rich realm of biodiversity?

It can be done by re-inventing the name 'terrace housing.' In our Matripolis proposal the 'terrace housing' is stepped back up a slope forming *true* terraces on which the rows of houses are arrayed. Access to all of them is provided by a gentle pedestrian ramp connecting all the residents to their common spaces and services at grade level.

Because the steps defining these terraces curve around to embrace the commons plaza, all the house facades inflect towards each other so that neighbors are more apt to get to know each other.

The terraces are designed to terminate at the level of the graded slope at each end. This slope merges with existing park land so that at any of six deck levels, hedgehogs, people and squirrels can wander freely, east and west, or up and down the ramp.

Not only is the local habitat thereby integrated but the human component is blended effortlessly into the mix. Bio-diversity here at last includes the human animal.

The Human Animal

> *We have virtually abandoned living in traditional societies. But this was the only way of life that humans knew for their first 6 million years on the planet.* – Jared Diamond

Our proposal sets the stage for a new kind of interaction between the human and non-human animal. It is not new for our species but new for inhabitants of modern cities.

Matripolis is designed in such a way that people's homes directly abut the commons. By 'commons,' we mean a space not just common to human residents, but common to other animals too. It is an outdoor space, predominantly green, devoid of motorized vehicles and the acres of hard surfacing they entail. Necessary paving for pedestrians and bikes is composed of porous material.

Some may argue that such a juxtaposition of, what used to be called 'Man' with what used to be called 'Nature,' is an impossible and quixotic dream and could never be reconciled with modern life in cities, except perhaps, for a privileged few.

We argue the contrary. The form of the proposal we presented is site specific but the principles on which it is based are quite generic. As the economy has become globalized so has the life style of the city dweller. Cultural differences have been largely ironed out by universal dependence on the products of the corporate system of mass production. We now have, unfortunately, a monoculture.

What are the principles on which we based our proposal?

They can be reduced to one principle—integrated habitat, or, more accurately, *re*-integrated habitat, for as Jared Diamond points out in the above quotation, we humans got used to living that way during our first 6 million years of existence.

All social animals associate with others of their own kind for their mutual benefit. Kropotkin calls this the predominant fact of nature. Human animals, given the freedom to do so, will naturally want to associate with their own kind for their mutual benefit.

Planners and architects should encourage them to do so, by removing obstacles, such as traffic streams cutting off private from public spaces. Ultimately, local communities should be given the freedom to govern themselves, deciding for themselves in community assemblies, for example, which streets within their territory, should be closed to traffic.

In so far as local communities form, organize and empower themselves, they should be able to institute cultures of sharing and mutual aid which will largely replace the market economy of waste and addiction that is the root cause of the present ecological and economic crises.

The Eco-Crisis

> *Our great psychological barrier to facing the problem of climate change is that we know it is a reflection of our technological use, misuse and waste of mined energy, which we can call industrialization; and that our many national forms of industrialization are each reflections cast in hardware, processes, systems and bureaucracies of our dominating ideologies of economic development. – Manuel Garcia Jr.*

The word 'economy' derives from the Greek 'oikonomia,' which means 'household management.' The word 'ecology' is compounded from the same root –the Greek word 'oikos' meaning 'house.' The crises we have brought upon ourselves therefore result from the way we have chosen to construct our 'house' and live in it.

Both words have expanded immeasurably from their original usage. We now understand 'economy' to embrace the whole world, the management of the sum total of all the household economies comprising all the settlements of all the nations on earth. And this management is largely invisible and certainly beyond the control of the individual householder.

Matripolis proposes a new way of 'managing the household'— at the community level. The community organizes itself as a larger household, incorporating all the individual households within its territory. The territory is well defined with clear boundaries formed—in this exceptional case—by *natural* features.

Just as it has a well-defined edge, so it has a well-defined center, which is, significantly, an *open* center—the 'agora.' All the homes focus on this space. It is as if, for example, all the 'café culture' that Jane Jacobs extols in Greenwich Village, is here plainly visible from each of the receding terraces. The commons 'invites' all the residents to participate in the activities in the commons, where they may see their friends amongst the crowd. People living in the community enjoy easy access to the commons. It is a community space but also a public space, equally friendly to visitors from neighboring communities.

The only entity that is firmly and forever excluded is the motorized vehicle.

Vehicular access is, of course, necessarily provided, but not in plain sight. What Matripolis illustrates, is that urban communities need to be pedestrian enclaves. In a typical urban condition, vehicles would be restricted to the boundary road and to service areas, and parking spaces adjacent to it.

But ideally, the front doors of all the houses should open directly onto community gardens. From these gardens, residents can sense the entire extent of their community, its gardens, its homes, and its commons. Then, even a child on a scooter can easily visit all parts of the collective home, unsupervised, and in complete safety.

Matripolis achieves this one-way, other urban communities could be re-planned to arrive at the same benefits, by whatever means would be appropriate to the site conditions.

We all place the highest value on our individual freedom, and we have developed an economic system that caters to our individual needs. One result of this system is that it generates a huge amount of waste. For example, it has recently been estimated that as much as 50% of food produced by agribusiness goes to waste. And this happens while 20% of the global population is malnourished.

Individuals organized as communities could eliminate, for example, food wastage, by setting up a composting system producing natural fertilizer, as Matripolis does. Some food could be produced within the community itself, and a community food coop could make an arrangement with local farms for bulk buying, so that little if any food would need to be obtained through super markets. This in turn would eliminate another whole world of waste that goes into packaging of food in small individual portions, made necessary by our present atomized living arrangements. And the same argument applies to manufactured products. Matripolis supplies hydro-electricity to all 500 residents. None of these householders could easily get themselves off the grid acting alone. As a community they can.

The objection is often raised that if we associated in communities our individuality, even our privacy, would be threatened. But this comes from a myopic view of the source of our freedom as individuals. For the majority of people, modern life involves a trade-off between free time and the wherewithal to acquire goods and services. The more we allow ourselves to indulge the former the less we will earn the latter.

To the extent a community self organizes to *share* products and services, the cost of living for member households will go down. This not only lowers the carbon footprint but could translate into more free time. That is to say, a turn from total private ownership to partial collectivization at the community level, would increase, not decrease, the free time and, therefore, the freedom, of the individual.

But a conservative critic would challenge this by asserting that the time saved by the individual through sharing of resources would be more than compensated by the debating time that would be required to reach consensus on the setting up and administration of each shared resource.

However, debating or conversing with our fellow communards, given that it would be a process leading to improvement in the daily lives of all, would not be seen as an imposition on the individual but rather as the restoration of a felt need for sociality which modernity has largely deprived us of. An expansion of our social lives would not be seen as a painful chore but a pleasant escape from the loneliness and alienation so widespread in our consumerist culture.

Economies of scale and scope are often invoked by economists to justify the incredible degree of concentration of industrial production that market forces have created. But it is rarely noted that those economies of scale and scope also operate for 'the consumer' at the community level.

For example, as Matripolis demonstrates, car dependence is completely eliminated. Many people could find work within their own community. Others could bike to work in the local neighborhood. For commuting, only very few would need to *own* a car and these could be parked alongside the coop cars available to the majority for use on special occasions. For the 500 households, then, perhaps 25 parking spaces would suffice. The same households in suburbia would probably require 10 times that number.

Our economic system *manufactures* everything, including food. And much of it is wasted. But the ecological system *grows* everything, and nothing is ever wasted, because decaying organisms always feed other organisms at a lower level of development. Harmonizing these two systems will be necessary if we are to resolve the eco-crisis.

Urban communities configured on the model of Matripolis, by enabling people to participate in the rational re-design of parts of the economy that affect them most directly, are formations that could contribute to this necessary harmonization.

As Montaigne wrote, 'Man cannot make a worm, but he makes gods by the dozen.' Our neo-liberal ideology has made a god of the free market and this has brought us to the brink of climate catastrophe.

The Crisis of Neo-liberalism

The idea of the sovereign individual lies at the heart of the neo-liberal ethic. Closely linked to this idea are others, such as—that markets are based on the principle of 'informed people making rational choices' and—freedom necessarily entails acceptance of the supposed law of nature: 'survival of the fittest.' This latter principle, wrongly attributed to Darwin, completely subverts what Darwin actually found, based on his extensive scientific observations.

> *'It is not the strongest of the species that survives, nor the most intelligent that survives. It is the one that is the most adaptable to change.'*

> *'In the long history of humankind (and animal kind, too) those who learned to collaborate and improvise most effectively have prevailed.'* – *Charles Darwin*

But a society composed of individuals who were *only* interested in themselves would not be a rational one, and would immediately break down. Likewise, a society in which only the fittest survived would imply that all the less fit would die. This is an equally nonsensical notion.

Yet we are governed by an economic system, the 'free market,' that is based on such principles. It is no wonder that it is so unstable, staggering through alternating cycles of 'boom' and 'bust.'

In such an environment the isolated individual is extremely vulnerable. In times of recession, the market may or may not deliver the goods the individual needs. But those needs are constant. He/she can buy the goods if she has enough money. But he/she is also part of the *labor* market and in times of recession there may be no available jobs.

States have put welfare provisions in place to compensate for the inevitable instances of market failure, but even these publicly financed systems are now under attack by the corporate elite, who seek to privatize as much of them as possible.

Matripolis proposes that people embedded in communities would be far better equipped to survive the vagaries of the markets. Temporarily unemployed individuals could provide child care for working parents. They could assist in food production and preparation. Individual problems, financial, medical, mental or of any other kind could be aired at the weekly general assemblies and sympathetic advice offered by a range of communards who may have experienced and solved similar problems in the past.

Many artifacts, appliances and tools, could be shared, and used according to an agreed upon planned schedule. This would dramatically reduce the number of these articles produced, sold, and individually owned.

It may be protested that the cumulative effect of such a 'reclaiming of the commons,' would have a disastrous effect on the economic system we have in place.

That is partly the point. We need to re-configure our whole means of production so that it ceases its parasitic growth at the expense of the environment. We are at a tipping point. We must restore balance or cease to be human. We must somehow institute a Steady State Economy, while we still have the chance.

Steady State versus Growth Economy

The logic of capitalism is that, other things being equal, maximum output equals maximum profit. An unregulated capitalist system must grow or die. Any CEO who would try to convince shareholders that he aims to lower production incrementally to reduce stress on the eco-system would rapidly find his corporation facing bankruptcy, unless similar policies were simultaneously imposed by his competitors. And this could only occur as a result of state regulation, an impossibility in to-day's political climate.

Even as early in the industrial revolution as 1857, John Stuart Mill was already commenting:

> '*I cannot ... regard the stationary state of capital and wealth with the unaffected aversion so generally manifested towards it by political economists of the old school. I am inclined to believe that it would be, on the whole, a very considerable improvement on our present condition.*'

More recently, in 1972, Arnold Toynbee wrote:

> '*More and more people are coming to realize that the growth of material wealth which the British industrial revolution set going, and which the modern British-made ideology has presented as being mankind's proper paramount objective, cannot in truth be the wave of the future. Nature is going to compel posterity to revert to a stable state on the material plane and to turn to the realm of the spirit for satisfying man's hunger for infinity.*'

And later in the same decade (1977) Herman E. Daly added this:

> '*sufficient wealth efficiently maintained and allocated, and equitably distributed—not maximum production—is the proper economic aim.*'

Current ecological and economic woes indicate that the world has overshot its sustainable natural limit of growth. We are entering a period of transition to a lower level of production and population growth. This needs to be followed by a period of orderly descent where production and population decline. And finally, this should achieve, at some point in the future, a new kind of global homeostasis, where a smaller, stable, and more agrarian human population lives in harmony with a rich diversity of other species, and enjoys cultural, moral and spiritual growth—but not the material kind. (H. T and E. C. Odum 2001).

Matripolis proposes a new kind of model urban community as an important part of achieving the necessary economies during the transition phase. As a site-specific application, its built form is unlikely to be repeated, but its social organization is theoretically replicable in all residential zones of large cities.

The leading idea here is that people should collaborate with their neighbors to take charge of their own environment, social, economic, as well as physical, where they live. They should then strive, over the years, to approximate local autonomy, free from the dictates of the international market.

Capitalism, the car, and the destruction of urban culture

The advent of the railways represented something completely new and incomparable to any previous influence on the form of cities in any part of the world at any date prior to the 19th century.

It was the first time in the history of civilization that a mechanical movement system was adopted that required its own dedicated network of tracks completely separated from the streets and roads that had up until then accommodated pedestrian and wheeled traffic.

The stations the railway system required had to be sited as close as possible to the historic cores of the cities they served. Each station covered a footprint far larger than any previous building type. The miles of track leading into and out of the stations, because it all had to be built, more or less, at the same level, regardless of the local topography, required extensive engineering structures of a scale unseen since the Roman aqueducts.

And all this had to be somehow accommodated in the heart of the historic, pedestrian dominated city. It could only be done at a cost, and one of the major costs was the disruption of local communities. The common expression 'from the wrong side of the tracks' says it all.

Big business needed the railways to move large volumes of extracted material from the mines to the factories and manufactured products from the factories to the cities where the consumers were concentrated. As a side benefit people could now travel quickly from city to city.

With the explosion of urban populations during the early years of the 19th century, systems of mass transit were needed. These were at first provided by horse drawn omnibuses. Later in the century, these were improved by laying down railway tracks in the center of major streets. It was found that horses could pull much heavier loads if wheels were of steel running on steel tracks. The next important development was the harnessing of electric power, and the replacement of horse drawn carriages by trams. But this did not occur until close to the end of the century.

The 20th century soon brought on the ever-increasing flood of privately owned cars powered by internal combustion engines, which to this day constitutes the main problem that cities (and the environment) have to deal with.

There is colossal waste in a system of transportation in which four-seated vehicles usually run with only one seat occupied. This is compounded when we consider the average car remains parked for most of every day and night. Wherever it remains parked for those hours, it is occupying urban space which is useless for any other purpose.

But it is not just modern transportation systems that destroyed the city as a coherent entity, but the whole economic system, the whole way of life that it supports—or in some cases, imposes.

Laissez faire capitalism has been weakly regulated by local authorities. This regulation has mainly taken the form of granting permission to build only specified building types in areas zoned for them. The consequence has been the chopping up of the city into specialized enclaves—that is to say, *segregation* of one urban function from another—the opposite of integration. The original motivation was public health, but ultimately it became more to do with protecting land values. This has been socially divisive.

One way of viewing the modern city is as a patchwork of different districts assigned to two different classes. One kind of district houses those who own their own homes, cars etc. Another kind of district, separated at some distance from this, contains workplaces and high-end shopping facilities for these kinds of people. A third kind of district is for renters, few of whom can afford to own cars. But here. there is no segregation of the housing from the shopping and 'blue-collar' workplaces that serve the wider market. They are all mixed together because land values are low and need to stay that way in order to provide affordable rents.

This adjacency of multiple uses that occurs in the low rent districts might have been advantageous if it had not been for the fact that these districts inevitably become fragmented by fast moving traffic of all kinds, passenger, freight, road and rail.

Now that the streets have been permanently pre-empted by fast moving vehicular traffic, there is a need to provide separate traffic free outdoor space, if the integrity of communities is to be restored in the modern city. Prior to the invasion of the car, the streets in high density residential areas of cities performed other functions than circulation. They often provided the only common space where adults could congregate for all sorts of purposes, formal or informal, and where children could safely play.

Integrated habitat, means, amongst other things, the condition where children of all ages can run safely in and out of their homes without adult supervision. The outdoor commons are the place, like the ancient Greek agora, where community identity is formed. It should be a place of peace and security, hospitable to people of all ages, and even to other forms of life. In Matripolis we have tried to apply these principles.

Self-empowered urban communities

World events occurring in the last two years since our proposal was presented have only reinforced the relevance of the message we attempted to convey.

Systemic change, of the kind clearly needed to avert climate catastrophe, will not be initiated by governments. History shows that significant social change only occurs as a result of mass movements from below, to which, then and only then, governments react, by passing appropriate legislation.

The Occupy Wall Street (OWS) movement may be the beginning of such an awakening (Chomsky 2012). It started by protesting the grotesquely skewed distribution of wealth in which 1% own the same amount as the remaining 99%. Significantly it set up its own self-help services in the camps it set up. Similar temporary self-help communities then sprang up spontaneously across the globe.

After the first wave of police repression it dispersed but continues to be active while avoiding the glare of publicity, for now. It has, for example, successfully averted individual foreclosures by drowning out with noise attempts by bank representatives to auction off their properties.

In the aftermath of the mega-storm Sandy, members of Occupy Sandy Relief have organized soup kitchens and delivered other kinds of emergency aid to thousands of flood victims beyond the reach of FEMA and the Red Cross. Some Occupy activists have found themselves rescuing policemen and their families on Staten Island who had previously been dispatched by the City of New York to evict them from Zucotti Square.

As the severity of the crises reaches the awareness of the general public, there are increasing signs that people are seeking alternatives to mindless consumerism. Co-operatives, co-housing, and intentional communities are gaining popularity and the Transition Towns movement is promoting the revitalization of urban communities.

The need to downsize costs of living and the imperative to reduce our carbon footprints, both favor the *sharing* of space and facilities, such as those formerly divided up between each individual, living in isolation. But the real gains for the social animals we are, is that we are brought back into a much more natural condition of association with our fellow beings. We are sure to be happier, if, while not giving up a modest private domain, we are accessible to the company of others of the same inclination, on a day to day basis.

And this return to a more natural condition of association, includes association with other species, plants, birds and animals. We already show this instinct with our private gardens and pets. But an urban condition where a small private front garden immediately abuts a larger community garden offers far greater flexibility of use.

Neighbors can jointly plan and cultivate areas where children of different ages can play with those of other families, areas where old people can sit and chat in the shade of a tree, areas for permaculture, for public art, and so on.

In Matripolis, access to the houses is through these green areas, increasing the chance of casual meetings between people of all ages. This is likely, over time, to build increasing community solidarity. In addition, in our example, there is the added benefit of direct connection of the gardens with wilderness areas.

We have shown an ideal condition where a new kind of social entity colonizes new territory. Because it is a brown-field site there are no pre-existing buildings to be planned around. There is a tabula rasa, in which a model community is imagined occupying a purpose-built structure in a specific site situation.

But there are many principles involved here that could benefit existing communities, within the constraints of the existing building stock.

Matripolitan principles applicable to urban communities

Our competition entry, Matripolis, shows a purpose-built project that demonstrates a new kind of social entity: a constructed environment where residents can easily interact with each other and with other nature. We propose this as an appropriate way of developing a typical brown-field site left vacant by an outsourced ship building industry on the River Tyne.

We will now consider to what extent Matripolis can be taken as an appropriate model for transforming cities, generally, into eco-cities. We do not suggest the replication of its *physical* structure—only its *social* structure.

୶

The ways in which a community comes to define itself are many and varied. The different modes are not mutually exclusive within any given municipality and the timing of their emergence will depend on the different local conditions, physical, social, economic, and psychological.

For any citizen to identify themselves as belonging to a community, there must be a territory defined by a boundary. The boundary could be legally defined, such as the city ward, or the postal code. The strongest sense of definition occurs when all the boundaries of a territory are demarcated by physical barriers. These could be entities such as a river, a railway embankment, a motorway or arterial, a major bus route, or a change of use such as residential to industrial.

To be viable, every community must also have a center. If it does not have one, the community's first task is to create one. The reason for this is that residents of a territory must meet together in general assembly before they can agree to form a true community. In many cases, centers already exist and do not have to be created. There may be a pub, a couple of shops, a disused church, a vest pocket park, or even a vacant lot. A sense of being at the focal point of a community can occur just as well at the boundary as in the physical center of the territory. Centers at the edge could, in some cases, be shared with adjacent communities.

The community, having established its boundary and its general assembly point, can then, in theory, begin to develop its policies for self-governance. And these will naturally be different for each community.

But one common goal that will likely be the conclusion with regard to the physical re-planning of the territory concerns vehicular and pedestrian traffic separation.

The long-term goal of every general assembly is likely to be to confine vehicular circulation to the boundary, with cul-de-sacs off the boundary road to service the housing. Interleaved with these service roads there need to be pedestrian/bike paths radiating out from the largely traffic free center to the other side of the same housing units (the Radburn system).

Participatory planning is generally accepted as a desirable way of bringing about physical change in the city. Today, it is common for the city planning department of big cities to prepare draft plans and then present them to an invited assembly of citizens to comment on. Citizens thus 'look over the shoulder' of the professionals as they do their work.

What is suggested above is radically different. The planning program should emerge from the discussion of the needs and desires of the community, meeting in general assembly. Through direct, face to face democracy, they will pass, by majority vote or by consensus, on each item of change required to correct physical flaws in the environment as they perceive them. Only then would environmental designers, preferably living in the community, be called in to advise on technical matters and implementation strategies.

The same principle applies to other professional services. The primary reason for the enormous success of the Cuban health care system is that doctors live in the communities they serve.

Newly empowered communities would find ways to plan other aspects of their lives, at present too much controlled by professional and institutional entities far removed from their day to day concerns. Communities may find that aspects of education, medical care, and the supply of good, healthy and fresh food are inadequately taken care of by the state and/or the 'free' market—in their particular case.

Demand side economics—planning versus markets

One of the reasons for the overgrowth and waste involved in the consumer society, that we have become, is adherence to the 'supply side' theory of economics promoted by Milton Friedman and now taken as gospel within the dominant sphere of the 'Washington Consensus' (which includes the Westminster Consensus, and many others, globally).

In its favor, we have to acknowledge, that the theory, up until very recently, has been spectacularly successful in achieving its main aim. That is to say it has translated into an exponential rate of *growth* (measured in GNP).

It is undeniable that much of this growth has been good for mankind, leading to less burdensome, healthier, and longer lives for many men and women. GNP however, is a gross measure of *all* kinds of products. It makes no distinction between those that are designed to cure and those that kill.

Neo-liberal theory is that the capitalist entrepreneur invents, produces and promotes a product, and supplies it to the consumer. It is supply side economics. In practice, if products are discarded, wasted or consumed before they have served their purpose, this is good for business. The fashion industry, drug addiction, warfare, and advertising are all institutions favorable to repeat sales and steady capital accumulation.

But as we have shown above, there is an urgent necessity for the rate of growth of the global economy to *slow down*, then to contract, until it reaches a steady state within the limits set by the terrestrial capacity to renew vital eco-system 'services' (Daly 1977).

Of course, this entails that the human population follows the same course: a slowing down of the rate of growth followed by a contraction to the point where our numbers can be sustained without overloading the bio-capacity of the earth.

Population projections have shown that this decline in numbers is actually likely to happen anyway as a by-product of the spread of modernity. Wherever women become emancipated and empowered to make their own life decisions, as long as reliable contraceptives are available, statistics show that populations will tend to remain stable or even decline.

The problem to be addressed is not one of numbers of people, but of a deeply embedded economic system designed for, and functioning as, a giant engine of capital accumulation. Left to itself, it cannot do anything but grow. Even if the number of consumers declined, profits would not. The system would rapidly invent, produce and promote new irresistible gadgets that people would be made to feel they cannot live without.

Would a 'demand side' economic system be appropriate for a period of contraction just as the 'supply side' system has catapulted the economy of growth?

It would seem reasonable to suppose that it would. But, in that case, how would consumer demand be expressed and transmitted to the producers?

Specialization has increased as a result of accumulating scientific knowledge. The average citizen finds herself increasingly dependent on artifacts, systems, and institutional edicts that she can have no way of understanding. Most people who use computers, for example, have not the faintest idea of how they work. Even when switching on a light, we take it on trust that the light will go on because we assume that someone who knows about electricity has provided the system we use.

One result of this increasing dependence on things we don't understand, is an increasing sense of helplessness and passivity. As long as the market provides us, as atomized individuals, with the things we have come to feel we need, we are content.

It is only when the market fails us, as, for example, the labor market ceases to provide the job we need to give us access to most other needs, it is only then that we turn to others for help. We may first seek help from our own relatives. If we are union members, we go to them. We may find others in the same plight and go out in the streets and demonstrate, in desperation.

What we will probably not think of doing is voting out the ruling party in our nation state. The state is another big system we don't know much about. We know it rules us but it is so remote and distant from our everyday lives, its rules and procedures so complex, its representatives so often not inspiring of our trust, that we don't really believe we can make significant change at the local level via that route.

City governments are closer to us but again rather remote from local concerns. They themselves administer programs often required by central governments and therefore subject to funding constraints imposed from above.

In order to combat the debilitating effect of social alienation and disempowerment that modernity carries in its train, individuals are beginning to see the value, if not the necessity, of associating with others in affinity groups.

Existing affinity groups can be classified as follows;

1. Common interest based
2. Workplace based
3. Neighborhood based

These groupings are not mutually exclusive. An individual, in fact *all* individuals, could be ideally associated with all three. Such groups have attributes in common. They all must have some kind of definition of membership. There must be some kind of non-hierarchical organization with consensus decision making, or in the case of larger groups, direct democracy. They will need a dedicated building where they can all assemble to make these decisions.

Over a certain size, confederation with other groupings of the same category would necessitate representation. But it would defeat the purpose of group empowerment to transfer any kind of *authority* to a representative. They could only report decisions made in the general assembly of the parent group (Biehl/ Bookchin).

Matripolis suggests that an ideal community would contain elements of all three types of affinity. By bringing some workplaces back into the residential zone, some residents could walk to work, allowing more time to become available for cooperation with their own and other families.

Housing cooperatives, co-housing groups and cooperative business enterprises might all find a natural home in organized communities already attuned to values of mutual aid.

Our proposal, called The Matripole, is based on the belief that the layout and form of housing could be instrumental in breaking down the wall of distrust that our competitive, consumerist culture has built up between individuals, classes, races and demographics.

The car is banned. Cycles are the vehicle of choice, where walking for some particular trip is deemed too slow. All houses are accessed through community owned and cultivated green space, which includes edible landscaping as well as 'wildness' and 'weeds' for biodiversity and playgrounds. Children can run out of their home's front doors, through their small front yards and directly into play space, where they are more than likely to meet other children from different families, and, indeed, the young of many other species.

⚛

Through their children's contact, parents will inevitably be drawn together also. But since, in any case, the neighbors on the same deck will be responsible for the design, care, and maintenance of the landscape they share, there is a built-in element of self-interest to cooperate and work together for the common good. They will naturally require and acquire a commons space for meetings and discussions.

Towards the Elimination of Waste

Just as the wasteful and socially alienating aspects of car dependency are eliminated in our proposal the same principles are applied to the 'waste' products of normal life.

The concept of 'waste' is peculiar to our species and loses all meaning when applied to the rest of the biosphere. Every single naturally produced organic product, including the lifeless organism itself, is broken down by microbial action and fed back into the food chain. Even the gaseous emissions from breathing animals is absorbed by plant life which pays for this gift with oxygen enrichment of the air. It is a fair and proper exchange that would keep life in balance and the air clean if only it were not for human interference.

⚛

In the Matripole, organic kitchen waste and sewage is conducted down behind the seven deck levels to anaerobic digesters at ground level. The gaseous, solid, and liquid products of this process are all then put to good use: the methane for cooking, the liquid effluent and solid sludge (after further processing) for fertilizer at all levels of the Matripole.

❧

Air vents for exhausted air and soil vents from the units are conducted in buried flues to chimneys that move the carbon laden air by natural convection. Before being exhausted, however, this air is purified by running it through the array of greenhouses that line the top deck.

The development faces south across a bend in the Tyne River. The constant motion of the water enlivens the view from all units and provides a more distant view of the south bank. The occasional passing boats and ships adds another special character to the site.

But the flowing waters provide another benefit. All the electricity used in the Matripole is generated by underwater turbines and there is no need for connection to the national grid.

In fact, the Matripole is self-sustaining in every way and needs no city utilities at all.

Potentially, people could advance from an isolated state of being where occasional visits to the domain of other life are their only form of contact, to a state where our homes are juxtaposed directly to the homes of the other in a new integrity.

This will be integrated habitat in the fullest sense.

❧

Architectural design for an individual client involves analysis of the individual's present needs and desires. Environmental design (which includes urban design) by contrast, caters to an abstract client, the collective. It is based on guesswork more than analysis.

But these two approaches are really not so different. Both depend on history. The individual's perception of her present needs is an outcome of her past experience just as the designer's guesses are dependent on her knowledge of successful urban spaces that already exist.

Architects and environmental designers, who, in a sense, are always designing for future users, are governed and constrained by the past, as built.

But we live in a time of rapid change that is unprecedented. What good is designing for a future based on the past when the only thing we know about the future is that it will not resemble the past?

There seem to be only three choices:

1. Conserve.
2. Adapt.
3. Innovate.

A is the easiest and, for the majority, the most popular. But since almost all existing practices are unsustainable, it means that not facing up to the need for change will result in changes being forced on us by the nature of things—and these are most likely to be unwelcome changes.

However hard we may wish for continuity of the status quo, it would be irrational to keep doing something that we know is causing, for example, catastrophic climate change.

Therefore, A defaults to B.

We must adapt anyway. It's a matter of survival. But as with an injured person there are two phases of cure.

First, stop the bleeding.

Second, consider ways to ensure long term health, and implement them on a more extended time scale.

So, it turns out there are not three choices but only one rational one.

A is out. B and C are both in.

❧

We must phase out fossil fuels as fast as we can. Then start to re-structure society, all its institutions and their urban containers, for long term steady state. Why? Because we have a growth system. It has worked so well that we are now overgrown. This is the root cause of all our problems. You cannot regulate a system whose whole raison d'être is capital accumulation, to just carry on, but accumulate *less!*

But when I say 'we' who am I referring to? *Not* architects, designers and planners.

All over the world, the younger generation are stirring now. They have woken up. The long overdue reaction to big business has begun. They are a force of nature. We must not stand in their way. They will form their own general assemblies and re-invent democracy. New grass roots institutions will emerge, grow, and consolidate their power.

Only then will the time be right to re-build the city to house appropriately the post-revolutionary communes.

CHAPTER 7

ORGANICITY STRIKES BACK

The world is at a critical stage in the conflict between two systems: The Economic and the Ecologic. The business of the Economy is to maximize profits for a few humans. The business of the Ecology is to maximize life for all its constituent organisms, including the human. From the perspective of Economics, the Ecosystem is an Externality. From the Ecological perspective, the human Economic system is an Externality.

Hence the conflict. Ordinary human beings, internal to both systems, are sometimes forced to take sides. This presents us with Ethical dilemmas.

The two systems are not always in conflict. Some of our needs are met outside the profit system, for example, medical care (at least in UK). And some manufactured goods promote healthy living, for example, bicycles.

Today though, for the most part, the economic system is destroying the ecosystem. In so doing, civilization seems to be about to shoot itself in the foot. This big-brained linguistic animal knows it has made a monumental error, so why doesn't it change direction, immediately?

A major reason this presents great difficulties is that the Economic system we have devised, so successful in growing itself quantitatively, is 'regulated' by markets, not people. Normally it is impossible for it to act without a market signal. Externalities do not generate market signals. Destroying Indonesian rain forests for palm oil production is profitable, for example. Re-foresting

Indonesia would not be profitable, though it is probably the only way to save the orangutan from extinction. Restoring damaged rain forests is one of the essentials to absorb the excess carbon dioxide our system continues relentlessly to pump into the atmosphere.

Our economic system, which Chomsky has recently taken to calling Really-Existing-Capitalism (REC), differs from the classical ideal in one important respect, namely that it is supported in a major way by the State (and not just in China). It is an immense juggernaut of quantitative growth on a global scale.

How can we expect this system to change its nature, to go into reverse, to switch from expansion to contraction?

A mass movement from below may be beginning, with protesting youth in developed countries (the Occupy movement etc.). These are questioning the very principles of REC. Those least beholden to REC and those who have the most to lose from its predations are the indigenous people in developing countries. They are beginning to make their presence felt (the Bolivarian revolution in Venezuela, Rights of Nature in Bolivia and Ecuador, Idle no More in Canada).

There are a number of components to bringing about the urgently required peaceful revolution. All of them will need to be implemented, to greater or lesser extent, depending on the different local conditions:

a) Re-localization
b) Alternative institutions both economic and social.
c) Renewable energy
d) Closed loop systems of manufacturing, energy production and waste disposal.
e) Mutual Aid (MA) instead of Mutually Assured Destruction (MAD)
f) Return to soil-friendly farming practices.
g) Progressive reduction in meat eating.

Origins

Out of its physical deficiencies came the human animal's need to insulate itself from the environment in which all other animals flourished. No other animal-controlled fire, for instance, because no other animal needed to. Their fur kept them warm.

The artificial world it built, as a result, became increasingly separated from the rest of the biosphere. It fenced off a portion of the wilderness and farmed it. Everything expanded, including its sense of superiority. It imagined there was a God, and God had made it in His image. It thought of itself as something other than an animal, and fought to suppress and denigrate any natural sensation that arose within itself that it could not control.

The human animal developed the ingrained habit of extracting whatever it needed from the Earth, and its other life forms, to support its increasingly complex life style. This had already begun to damage the ecosystem long before the mid19[th] century. But at this point there was an explosion, a big bang that triggered an exponential rise in numbers, with all its parasitic effects, at a far faster rate than the natural system could accommodate.

This is sometimes described as the period of rapid *growth* made possible by the Industrial Revolution. But it is wrong to call it growth. It is more correct to call it rapid *accumulation*—of population, urbanization and capital.

Three ingredients were essential to making the Industrial Revolution possible.

They came into existence together at the same historical point. They still shape and control our lives.

They are:

a) Fossil fuel extraction on an industrial scale.
b) Machines and the related idea of factory mass production.
c) Capitalism in its early post-Mercantilist guise.

Marx focused on the issue of 'who owns the means of production?' But this question is only significant in the context of the assumption that property must always have an owner, whether it be private or public. But fundamentally, in our industrial age, the means of production consist of two elements, factory machinery and their operators.

In other words, term b) will underpin any imaginable future even if a) and c) are replaced. The issue of ownership is secondary. Everything a society uses could be considered part of the commons, if society chose to make it so.

Automation, carried to its logical conclusions, could replace the machine operators with other machines (robots). Then, all menial tasks would be performed by electro-mechanical operators. At last, the world would be free from class warfare. Instead of humanity being divided between the 'haves' and the 'have nots,' masters and slaves, owners and renters, creditors and debtors, there would be an aristocracy comprised of all humanity. Relaxing in freedom and living long lives exclusively devoted to developing their innate gifts to the limit of their capacity, they would be served with all their needs at the flick of a switch.

Although the above vision of heaven on earth is more plausible than the old one, of heaven somewhere else, it is flawed. To begin with the obvious flaw, not all human needs are factory made. Food for instance is grown, not manufactured. Present practices of factory farming are not sustainable and must be replaced. The recent experiment in manufacturing faux meat is an abomination and taking us in exactly the opposite direction of where we need to go.

The Organic versus the Machinic

On your imaginary Power Point screen, you will see projected two intersecting circles. In the left circle is written the word Organic and, in the right, Machinic. In the leaf shape where they intersect, written vertically, is the phrase Modern Humanity. The Organic is synonymous with the ecosystem, all organisms and their inter-relationships with each other, and with the natural environment. But crucially it includes the human organism and all its behaviours, institutions and relationships developed up to the Industrial Revolution—many of them co-existing with modernity. The Organic mode of being is growth, from a seed, through individual lives, that are always unique, though deeply connected, and the dying back into the soil of new growth in an endless cycle in which decaying life perpetually feeds new life. The Machinic, by contrast, is characterized by *dis*connection. Its power comes from the analysis and isolation of specific problems and by the design of means to solve them. It is not cyclic but linear. Typically, machinic processes start by extraction, and end in waste. It is strongest in dealing with problems in the terrain of physics and chemistry. It is weakest when dealing with life and living systems.

The Organic procreates while the Machinic reproduces, although these words are often used incorrectly in ordinary parlance.

What distinction are we making here and why is it important?

⟀

'Of that which we do not know we cannot speak' quoth Wittgenstein. He failed to add 'of that which we all know there is no need to speak.' Silence follows. And yet ... we all know that we have to eat to stay alive. Since humans are at the top of the food chain this shouldn't be a problem for us. But it is. Why?

Capital, in the over-developed world, has long since mechanized most of food production in its own interests. Knowing that profits flow most fully from addicted consumers, it concentrated on providing forms of food (and beverage) that *look* good on the supermarket shelves and *taste* good (especially when fried in fat by McDonald's). They were not concerned about the marketing of foods that actually *are* good as defined by independent health experts.

The most profitable food is junk food and that is why the supermarkets are full of it.

The negative results of Machinic Agriculture are many and a true accounting of them would fill a book. Here are a few:

a) Rapid destruction of the earth's remaining rain forest areas that perform a vital role in the hydrologic cycle and carbon absorption. Largely, this is being done to increase growing surfaces for the animal *feed* consumed by

b) a hugely bloated population of farm animals kept in vile and unhealthy conditions and suffering immense cruelty. They are just barely kept alive long enough to be ready for slaughter. No wonder their diseases are sometimes passed on to humans and other species.

c) Huge rise in obesity and obesity-related illnesses, especially among children in the over-developed countries like ours.

d) Degradation and loss of top soil due to the substitution of Machinic chemicals for the manure, compost, and decaying organisms that would build up top soil as a normal function of the Organic cycle.

e) Draining out of aquifers due to excessive water use required by Machinic Ag. Some of these aquifers are in the non-replenish-able category.

If we would reform our economic system to bring it back into a rough balance with the natural systems in which it is embedded, we will need to isolate the concept of the Machinic in order to understand where and how the vital Organic connections have been severed by inappropriate expropriations.

Organicity is not different from the anarcho-communist aspirations of its 20th century forbears. It includes them, but adds to them consideration, love and compassion for the other lives and living systems which walk fly and swim on the planet we share with them.

It is often remarked that 'we need to get back closer to nature.' In the modern city, we have surrounded ourselves with artificial structures and hard impermeable surfaces. Large metallic objects incessantly speed on their way. A visitor from another planet would probably assume that cars were our dominant species. Or perhaps that they were the babies of the buses. The alien might at first overlook the fact that these creatures eventually come to rest in parking lots, that from inside them small parasitic organisms emerge. and dive into large squared-off ant hills (or so it might interpret our buildings).

The public domain in most modern cities is 90% occupied by paved surfaces for vehicular movement and parking. For the disenfranchised foot born citizen the remaining 10% is confined to disconnected pieces skirting the 'blocks' of buildings, which of course are overwhelmingly *not* public domain, but privately owned.

Who is the metropolis supposed to serve, the ordinary citizen or only the owners of cars and property?

LETTER TO TINA

Hi Tina,

I had some thoughts about Tuesday night's conversations, particularly what you and Chris had said.

You said you came from a communist background but that your core belief, now, is that people are born with a propensity to get along with each other. You gave as an example your instinct *not* to bat your neighbour's annoying child over the head. But I hope you would agree that this child will probably soon learn, from its peer group, how not to, and why not to, behave in an offensive manner?

Most of us learn from an early age that the best way to get what we want is to make ourselves lovable in the eyes of those who can provide it. This is typically the case within the family and has been described by Graeber as baseline communism. Most other animals live the same ethic in bringing up their young. So, it goes very deep.

But in our consumer society mutual aid stops at the front door. As soon as we are in the street, another ethic prevails. You get what you pay for. No more and no less (actually you get *less*— unless you are buying from a non-profit organization).

This personal belief of yours would have been shared by Marx or any other person of socialist or left persuasion, would it not? The Communist Party itself, as invented by Lenin, recognized the withering away of the state and its succession by networks of autonomous communes (soviets) as its ultimate goal. But Lenin was arguably not wrong in concluding that the historical conditions, post WW1, required the imposition of central authority and the rapid formation of a Red Army to defend the revolution, even in its incomplete stage.

The ultimate goal of communists is that the state be replaced by networks of communes. Here, the social animals we are, could cooperate, in a spirit of mutual aid, in a social space in which to do so. This group process, governs itself up to a certain size, by consensus, in larger aggregations, by direct democracy and at municipal and all higher levels through delegates, not representatives.

The *ultimate* goal of Communism is identical to the *immediate* goal of Anarchism. They differ, radically, only in their team strategy for arriving at the final kick into the goal.

Anarchists trust people to behave in socially responsible ways if given the freedom to form intentional communities, communes, affinity groups, or work syndicates, which are fully empowered to form and regulate themselves, and to network themselves in larger aggregations.

anarchists
are communists
who won't wait
for the State.

Many aspects of modern technology support and facilitate the decentralization of power. It takes little imagination to see that Internet networks, for example, could connect people with needs to those with the ability to cater to them, in short order. And this could be achieved automatically, without the need for any central control from any established authority. The global network of postal services is all smoothly interconnected, not by the command of any authority, but simply because everybody gains by such integration.

However, according to Glenn Greenwald,

> *The promise of the Internet was that it would liberate people and bolster democracy, but it has become a tool for suppression and control. In fact, it is one of the most powerful instruments of control ever invented. The most essential challenge we face today is related to the*

real effect of the Internet. Will it impart power to people and liberate them, or will it impart more strength to the centers of power and help them oversee, control and suppress the population? That is the struggle of our generation, and it has yet to be decided.

CHAPTER 8

MIXED METAPHORS:
A PLAY IN ONE ACT

We must not throw the *Baby* (freedom) out with the *Bathwater* (state)
but we tend to ignore the *Elephant* (economy) in the *Room* (ecology)

*The curtain parts to reveal four characters seated at a table; two
women, a man, and an elephant. Room's costume is modeled on the
goddess Gaia, but her dress is rather tattered. Baby is dressed like
the statue of Liberty. Bathwater looks like President Obama and
Elephant is the stereotypical capitalist with dark suit, top hat, and
smoking a cigar which he holds in the mandibles of his trunk. The
stage set is a simple room with two windows, one with Opportunity
written by it and the other with Time Left. There are thousands of
manufactured consumer objects scattered all over the floor (TV sets,
appliances, Ipads, computers, cameras etc.)*

Room: Will somebody please open the window? It's so stuffy
in here. What a gassy elephant you are!

Baby: I'll do it. Which window though, the window of
opportunity or the window of time, the short time in
which scientists say we must curb emissions?

BW: Baby, you're a dreamer. There are no windows and
even if there were, what's out there is just an irrelevant
externality. Let's get the Elephant moving again and

after that maybe consider what we can do about his unfortunate flatulence.

Elephant: I'm all for that. I'd love to be active again, crashing through the jungle and tearing up trees by the roots, just for the fun of it. Ah, to feel my power again, to push back Room's walls so Baby can have more space to play in. I love it.

Baby: What good is space if you leave us no time to play in it? We have no time left after spending it all on feeding you so you can provide us with toys. Look they are lying all over the floor! We can barely navigate between them. Other animals are much more fun to play with than your toys, anyway.

Room: Elephant is killing off other animals and expropriating their habitat to make room for more toy factories. You are not a real elephant and not even an appropriate metaphor. You are a Machinephant.

BW: Enough name calling. We will all drown in a sea of mixed metaphors unless we get one thing straight. The four of us are all in the same boat. We must sink or swim together. Woman the life boats. Stop moving the deck chairs on the Titanic.

Elephant: I say full steam ahead. Damn the torpedoes. Hull down, folks.

Baby: 200 years ago they told me that if I put my faith in the free market, I would flourish but now Elephant has everything and I am a debt slave. How come?

BW: Elephant lent you the money to buy yourself a house. Of course, you have to work hard to pay him back, and of course, with interest. There is no alternative. Well I suppose you could always rent. The state can provide, if you're too poor to buy. But everyone has to work. Unless they're dead—or very sick.

Room: I *am* very sick because Elephant keeps bleeding my guts. You are a bunch of delinquent children. Your future progeny will pay dearly for your selfishness and blind tunnel vision (I can mix metaphors too).

Elephant: Don't blame me. I only provide you with what you want. That's what markets are for. We are all complicit. You have your I-pads and I have my yachts.

The two women get up from the table and come up front stage. In the background Elephant and BW pull out a game of Monopoly and start playing—with intermittent laughter, nudges, winks and rib digging.

Room: Come with me Babe, let's leave these two to their machinations. Perhaps we can begin to solve this problem if we work together. You love me, don't you?

Baby: How should I not love you? You're my mother, in a manner of speaking. Still …

Room (interrupting): So, you know how I'm suffering and you want to help me don't you?

Baby: Ye...es. But …

Room: Why are you so ambivalent?

Baby: I know you made me what I am. You shaped my biology and fired up my desires. You instilled me with basic goodwill toward others. You are also the source of my ethical and aesthetic values, (although we often wrongly attribute these to the religions we have invented). In one sense, I am simply the fulfillment of these urges that manifest the force that drives us all. Free will is simply the measure of your essence, Room, in every individual.

Room: You flatter me Babe. I am not conscious of anything so high and mighty. I have simply evolved a method that ensures uniqueness in every new-born, immense diversity, and the flourishing of any life form that can fit itself in somehow with pre-existing living systems. Individuals are of no interest or importance to me. The system as a whole is of vital interest to me, however, and every individual's life will be negatively affected by its breakdown.

Baby: Therein lies my problem. *You* are not conscious, but we animals *are* conscious, *as individuals,* and only as individuals. We aspire to freedom from *all* constraints, be they imposed by tyrannical bosses, stupid laws, outdated customs or even our own biology. We seek transcendence.

Room : You've lost me. I don't know what you're talking about.

The Monopoly game is abandoned and the players wander over to join the women. BW puts his arm around Baby. Elephant wraps his trunk affectionately around Room's neck. She violently throws it off and walks ostentatiously to the other end of the row so that Baby and BW separate her from Elephant.

BW: You see, Baby and me are not so far apart. She lets me put my arm around her. Don't even think about throwing me out. She needs me, because I am the only agency that can ever control the rapacity of Elephant. We need to put Elephant on a diet until he shrinks to a size that fits in Room without asphyxiating her. To do that we will need a host of baby elephants, little machinephants to serve Baby directly with her needs and wants.

Elephant: To suggest putting me on a diet is reactionary and flies in the face of technological progress. You people have no idea what visions of luxury are in store for us if we follow the logic of machine production. We will be an aristocracy served by robotic slaves. They will make everything for us in factories including all our food and drink, unless by then we have replaced all our malfunctioning biological parts with replaceable metal and silicon components. Room can go to hell. Who needs all those animals and plants when we can make perfectly reliable artificial substitutes? Too hot—universal air conditioning. Clean water—sea water distillation.

Room: This is your moment of truth, Humanity. Strike out this madness with me now or forever after witness the inexorable slide to extinction for all life on earth!

Room and Baby pick up Elephant, protesting, and carry him to the Window of Opportunity.

Elephant : But you need me … (in a weaker voice) don't you?
Baby: Go and breed a herd of baby machinephants and slim yourself down. Then we might let you all back in.

They throw Elephant out the window. Then all three walk around the stage picking up many of the appliances, gadgets and toys and throw them out the other window. The few remaining objects are lined up in two neat rows. As the humans hold hands and with smiling faces skip and dance down the row from back to front of stage,

The curtain falls

CHAPTER 9

SUMMARY STATEMENT

DIAGNOSIS

Life on earth is in deep trouble because one species has proceeded on the false assumption that it has the moral authority to exploit all extra-human attributes of earth exclusively for its own benefit.

It has discovered, perhaps too late, that humanity is only one part of a living mutually interacting whole.

PROGNOSIS

There is an extreme likelihood that our dominant paradigm of endless growth will destroy the terrestrial environment as the haven for life that it has been.

There is still a possibility of changing our economic system to harmonize with, instead of disrupting, the ecosystem.

PRESCRIPTION

1. As individuals, learn the truth
2. Form affinity groups
3. As groups, form networks of groups
4. Through networks, organize for action
5. Act

CHAPTER 10

PRU'S Q'S, AND DOB'S A'S

Pru: If organicity is a self-regulating system, what has caused this unbalanced situation? Self-regulation has failed or does correction operate in a longer term?

The system in which organicity operates is the *eco*system. The loss of balance is brought about by the impact of another system, the human *economic* system. It too is supposed to self-regulate through free markets. Unfortunately, in practice, free market theory, which is supposed to produce the greatest good for the greatest number, has resulted in something like its opposite—the greatest good for the smallest number. But apart from this failure of the market-based system itself, there is the additional problem of its failure to synchronize its own operation with that of the ecosystem, which operates on entirely different principles. We humans are caught in the middle, trying to live out our destiny as social animals while enmeshed in mechanisms of our own devising.

Pru: You need to distinguish between organicity and Gaia theory. Gaia theory has proved to be popular and scientifically testable. Now widely accepted.

My understanding of Gaia theory may not be as good as yours. But here is my reflection on what I do understand of it.

The whole earth is a living being, an organism, not different in principle from each of the organisms that constitute the biosphere, except it is the sum total of all earthly life forms, interacting in the same way that the organs of each body interact to constitute a single organism at a higher level of organization.

I don't buy it—for the following reasons:

1. The stimulus/response test works on life forms and also works on Mother Earth. For example, too much CO_2 in the atmosphere causes earth temperature to rise like an animal with fever. *But stimulus/response is not the only attribute of living things*—a big mistake made by the Behaviourists.

2. The physical embodiment of life requires:
   a. Containment in a membrane that separates an interior from an exterior environment.
   b. Means of drawing in energy from the exterior, processing it internally and expelling it in chemically changed form.
   c. An instinctive drive to live, to associate with others of its own kind and to procreate.

None of these vital signs could apply to Gaia. She has no skin. She is all exterior and no interior. She does not eat, breathe, love or have sex. She has billions of children but no husband. Are we to imagine she is in touch with other living planets?

Pru: If organicity is a field like electricity/magnetism then it should be measurable (physically testable) and maybe even composed of force carrying particles. If it is conceptual or metaphorical then this is not as crucial.

Organicity is a noumenon, not a phenomenon. That is to say, it is something not directly sensed, but inferred from what we do sense. The life that is palpable in any living animal we see before us is inexplicable in terms of any physio/chemical account of cause and effect. It demands a field theory to explain it. Just as magnetism demands a field of its own. Gravity even more so. Even if we found a graviton the mystery would only intensify. A shower of particles can be understood as pushing an impacted object. But how could it *pull*? Sheldrakes's concept of a morphic field coming from a highly accredited biologist is the closest cousin to Organicity I know.

Pru: If life (biosphere) exists as a web of interconnections at various levels then e.g. food chains are part of it—predators and preyed upon species. Humankind appears to form the top predator level—both consciously and unconsciously? Hence the desire for domination or cowed acceptance of others domination?

Consider grass, antelopes and lions. A herd of antelopes eats the grass while also fortifying it with manure. The lions eat some of the older, younger, weaker or sicker members of the herd. All three species have the urge to live and proliferate. The interaction of the three makes for greener healthier grass, faster and healthier antelopes, and ever more fierce and cunning lions.

What at first looks like 'nature red in tooth and claw' is really a form of mutual aid. But because humans have a much more extensive form of consciousness, we are bound to reject the cruelties of the lower forms. We should eat low down on the food chain. And try to curb the carnivorous impulse.

My wife successfully turned our cat into a vegetarian, and its health improved.

Pru: Intra and inter species dynamics often result in competition for resources between different species and individual members. Perhaps competition/co-operation works at many levels in an uncoordinated manner?

There is, of course, both cooperation and competition throughout nature, but I am persuaded (by Kropotkin) that cooperation predominates among non-linguistic species at least.

I see evidence of this from my balcony. Over three seasons of gull watching I have witnessed predominant love and caring between mates. Challenges are very frequent, especially at the start of the mating season but they are invariably dealt with by a gesture of 'shove off,' which is invariably obeyed. I have never once seen an actual fight, let alone violence or injury. On the other hand, they occasionally torture, slowly kill and clumsily eat, a smaller bird of a different species.

This year there was a dysfunctional pairing. One of them was being very selfish and unreasonable to its mate. So, one day five or six gulls appeared out of nowhere. They all literally put their heads together to see what was the matter.

Pru: Will increase in information and awareness lead to the discovery and respect for our deepest values, and what are those values?

The deepest value anyone can have is Freedom. Because without it the exercising of any other value is blocked. Freedom means freedom to do what I want. Most people in this country, barring those who are unemployed or half starving, feel they *are* free. Even those who spend long hours in a job they don't like feel they are free—to find another job. They cannot imagine a society that is not divided into two classes, employers and employees. The words 'employ' and 'use' are synonyms. Why must there be two kinds of humans—the users and the used? There does not need to be. All work could be carried out by a fraternity of equals working together cooperatively. So, in order to have true Freedom, we need Equality and Fraternity also. But Freedom is the meat in the sandwich (bad metaphor).

> *As long as man accepts the authority of society over himself, he accepts the authority of traditional concepts, traditional patterns of behaviour, whether they are moral patterns of behaviour, religious patterns of behaviour or political and economic patterns of behaviour.*

As long as he accepts the authority of patterns of behaviour, he will never be free. – Vimala Thakar

Pru: Is organicity descriptive / predictive / normative? It seems to be all of those? Is it a Theory of everything?

It's not a theory of everything. It could be the philosopher's 'hard problem' in a different guise. There are obviously living organisms around and there is also consciousness or mind.

What is life, mind, consciousness? It is that which is absent from a dead organism. I call it organicity.

Pru: You sketch out a possible progressive path but what does it involve? Gradual change in a direction? A dialectic confrontation of opposing political and value systems? Unfolding disaster scenario?

We are getting 'blowback' from aspects of technology that have proved damaging to the environment. Our predicament is that our socio/economic system has grown so fast that we are heavily invested in it to the extent that alternative models cannot be devised, tested, and implemented fast enough to deflect runaway climate change. This exponential spurt of growth has been a result of two (bad) choices we as a species made:

1. Fossil fuel dependence, on the part of the many.
2. Exploitation of this fact by the few.

Regression and progression are not useful concepts any more. Unsustainable progress is not progress but is also not regress. We can't go backwards. We need 'steady state' in terms of population and 'resource use' (horrible phrase). We can combine this with immense progress in terms of knowledge acquisition, cultural production and the arts, especially the art of living naturally, which we have lost.

Pru: How does the bipolar organic/machinic division situate within the organicity systems approach? Is the Eros/Logos polarity a grand simplification of saying there are conflicting desires and many ways of thinking about things? For instance, is the 'architectonic' machinic or organic? Where does the inorganic reside?

This is difficult. I have not completely worked it out.

Linear versus lateral thinking.

Both our means of production and distribution are products of left brain, rational, mathematical calculation.

Means of production of goods – Identify a human need
  – Design a machine to satisfy it
  – Build another machine to make clones of that machine
  – Employ humans to run the manufacturing machine.

Means of distribution – Money. To the extent you have it you can buy stuff, including machines.

Means of production of money – Financial services industry. Banks.

Other important artificial/machinic concepts that could be changed:
  – Ownership of the means of production by any other than the producers (workers and managers but not shareholders) themselves.
  – Usury
  – Market fundamentalism

Most advanced stage of capitalism – USA (per capita wealth highest in the world)

Current statistics USA 2013.
Percentage of population living in poverty   – 50%

Number of individuals whose combined wealth equals the wealth of this 50%:

$$- 400$$

Real percentage of effectively unemployed $- 33\%$

Machinic thinking underlies machinic practice. Machinic thinking goes along with patriarchy, hierarchy and class warfare.

We need to start again in a holistic way.

In *space*
we need to consider the impact on all elements of the biosphere before accepting any device for widespread human convenience.

In *time*
we should consider the past, the present, and the future.

To what degree are our present plans unconsciously influenced by the physical and institutional structures inherited from the *past* that are no longer fitting for us now?

In view of current state of knowledge, what must society do NOW?

To what extent are our present practices creating intolerable conditions for *future* generations?

It was the concept of organic architecture, which I did not originate, that inspired me to explore organic urbanism, which I did. Organicity is a meta concept that grew out of my critique of the built world.

CHAPTER 11

ORGANICITY—JUST IN TIME?

*... [U]nless there are rapid and substantial changes
in how human beings interact with and effect our
environment by the year 2030, we shall see the beginning
of extinction of the human race, animals and most plants
by the end of this (21ˢᵗ) century. – Kim Scipes*

The above quotation from an excellent, thoroughly researched, and copiously referenced article has just been published (December 2016). Its analysis of the problem can hardly be questioned because it is evidently true. Scipes also suggests the kinds of changes needed, but he admits that these should be subject to public scrutiny and might vary from region to region as democratic processes are activated in the different countries of the world, in different ways.

So 'rapid and substantial changes' are urgently needed in our human way of life, globally. This is a 'given.'

The question is why? Or rather, how come? Have we not made huge strides forward, especially since the industrial revolution? The march of mechanized progress seemed to be leading us to a utopia and now we are told, on the contrary, we are headed for a cliff.

The philosophical question being examined here is, how can the conscious pursuit of the good lead to the actual arrival of its opposite, the bad? Or, where was (and is) the hidden flaw in our thinking?

Unless we answer this question first, how can we be assured that the changes we rapidly impose on ourselves, will not lead us into some other quagmire, unforeseen, because we never properly analyzed what we did wrong in the first place?

If we are intelligent enough to send rockets to another planet, how come we can be so stupid as to simultaneously wreck our own?

The hubris of humanity

Ever since one primate species, homo sapiens, separated from its cousins, it has fostered the illusion that it is separate from nature.

We know now that all species are related and have co-evolved. But this was by no means obvious at first. Humans were poorly designed for survival compared with other animals. They possessed no built-in weapons to defend themselves. Balanced on two legs, they lacked the inherent stability of quadrupeds. Their bodies were inadequately insulated. They could not fly and they were poor swimmers. They found out about fire, which kept them warm, and made their food more digestible and tastier. They invented weapons that were even more effective killing aids than claws and teeth. They found they could kill other animals, cook and eat their flesh and make clothes out of their skins.

For all the natural deficiencies that the evolutionary process had endowed them with, it is amazing that they survived, but they did, because of one huge advantage that more than compensated for their physical shortcomings: their enhanced mental attributes.

The invention of language provided the one crucial advantage that no other animal has, the ability to accumulate and disseminate detailed knowledge throughout the tribe and across generations.

❧

From the invention of language followed a plethora of other inventions; useful tools, such as writing, ploughs, printing and computers, and useful ideas, such as the state, monarchy, enslavement and religion.

Tools, when freely provided to users, are useful to all, but ideas, such as those mentioned above, are only useful to one class of human, be he a state functionary, an aristocrat, a master or a priest. They are useful only in the sense that a privileged few can dominate and exploit the masses for their *own* use. And they do this by impressing on *all* members of society the *sacredness* of whatever version of the idea is imposed at any particular place and time in history.[37]

As a matter of course, if one class of human is accepted as being always superior to another, then a fortiori, other *animals* must be vastly inferior to the human animal. So much so, that they become seen as a different kind of being altogether, or not *any* kind of being: automata, on the Cartesian[38] model. They must have been put there to serve *us*. So, we proceed to work our will on them, and their natural environment. Their world is not our world. Look at us. We are *so* different!

But to imagine our species as standing apart from the ecosystem has proven to be an extremely dangerous illusion.

The Integrity of Nature

The notion that the universe is comprised of two completely different categories of entity, for example, life forms on one hand, and inert matter on the other, although universally assumed, as a matter of common sense, runs into difficulty as soon as we try to reconcile it with the findings of modern science.

Science tells us that life evolved on earth from an earlier lifeless phase. It goes on to say that, from the earliest appearance of small single cell organisms, gradually more complex organisms developed, plants, insects, reptiles, mammals, primates and 'finally,' humans.

Ordinary people can understand and accept this theory except for the first step in the process. How can life evolve from non-life? It didn't, answers the dualist. God inserted life into a lifeless universe. How was that possible, one asks? For God, all things are possible, replies the dualist. But this is not credible. If One was creating a universe and was mainly interested in living things, One would make sure the germ of life was present in the very stuff of the universe, so One wouldn't have to keep meddling with it. Because One is immortal and all powerful, why on earth would One go for half measures, providing the soil for the daffodil and its glorious flower, but withholding the seed, which One would somehow then have to provide in a special act of creation, on certain planets and at certain stages, so that things could get going.

Spinoza took the next step. No, he said. Nature is the whole package. It's all there. From now on we are all monists. The greatest scientist in the world concurred. Einstein said I believe in the God of Spinoza. But there is still another problem.

The mind/body problem

Even for dualists this is a seemingly irreconcilable problem. If individual minds partake of the universal Mind, how come they are demonstrably always tied and bound to individual bodies? How can two things so opposed, the absolutely non-material mind and the absolutely material body *ever* connect? Yet we are certain they do. Our experience of ourselves confirms this.

For the monist there is still a difficulty. But there is one way out. Suppose the mind is simply an *aspect* of the body. Could it be an epiphenomenon? I know that I exist in my body. A newborn infant surely knows that it exists, although it can barely be capable of thought, contra Descartes. I *feel* therefore I am. This would be closer to the mark.

The 'thinking thing' is a secondary phenomenon arising out of the 'feeling thing.'[39] So the solution to the mind body problem is simple. Minds do not exist—at least not separate from bodies.

Can we say that feelings or emotions pertain to the whole body, including the brain, whereas thoughts are purely cerebral?

Our use of language, as it so often does, has led us astray. Minds may be *conceived* of as a reality, but that does not make them *independently* real.[40]

What does exist, are organisms, at varying degrees of complexity, from humans, down to a hydrogen atom, an electron, and even a quark. All are co-dependent and co-evolving.

Each organism (Whitehead's 'actual entity') has a degree of free will and agency. At the subatomic level this reduces to a pulse of motivating energy, so that it is impossible to say whether it is a wave or a particle. It is neither or both, depending on by whom and how it is observed. As we move up the evolutionary scale, pulse becomes impulse, then sentience, then bodily feelings and at some point, a degree of consciousness (an epiphenomenon). Perhaps the point at which some degree of consciousness enters the system is where the first plant mutated into the first 'root free' life form, be it an insect or a mollusk. Arguably, to think at all, one needs a head. But there are forms of marine life, for example, that may contradict this argument.

What is the most parsimonious explanation for our existence? It is that we are one outcome of evolution, a natural process that pervades the infinite extension of space/time. By natural selection, combined with the seeming miracle of mutation, new life forms continuously emerge. We humans do happen to exist in this earth particle of the universe. We might have emerged in a completely different form, because novelty is what evolution continuously creates, through the agency of its ever-procreating life forms.

Pan-psychism and pan-experientialism

Charles Darwin said 'humans differ from other animals in degree but not kind.' Even Aristotle acknowledged that we are a kind of animal. So, if we have admitted that mind, *as a separate entity*, in humans, can no longer be maintained as a scientifically plausible reality, we must also acknowledge that it must be the same case, to a perhaps greater degree, in 'lower' animals. So, matter and mind are just words. Neither really exists independently. There should be a single word for mind/matter or body/mind.

So far so good. All living animals are entities that incorporate physical and mental properties. They have a physical and a mental pole. They are psychosomatic, through and through.

But both pan-psychism and pan-experientialism make much greater claims. The former would have us believe that all things, without exception, have minds. The latter distinguishes between compound entities on one hand and aggregates on the other. A compound entity is a self-regulating living unit; a form of life, an animal, insect or plant. An aggregate is an assemblage of atoms and molecules that are brought into being by external physical forces. For example, a rock is an aggregate that was formed by external forces such as gravity, wind, running water and so on.

But pan-experientialists claim that the fundamental particles of matter all the way down to the quantum level, possess a microscopic degree of sentience. So, although it is true that the rock qua rock may be said to be lifeless, it is nevertheless also true to say that it is composed of billions of molecules, atoms and particles that each has its own individual tiny spark of 'élan vital,' so to speak.

Growth, Movement and Change

What is it within a tree that impels it to grow? Whatever it is, it must be *within* the tree. It is acted on by outside forces but it reacts to exigencies in ways that cannot be completely determined by its genes. For example, its roots will wrap around a large rock and conform themselves to it, while still growing thicker in conformity with the overall enlargement.

Recent studies have shown that plants seem to be especially sensitive in the tips of their roots. They have even been known to communicate with other specimens of their own kind via fungal spores connecting their root systems. They even seem to practice mutual aid! Trees in one part of a forest rich in some anti parasite chemical have transmitted through the same root system some of this chemical to other individual trees of the same species, not so endowed, that are being attacked by such a parasite.

So, it is not too much of a stretch to accept that trees, and by extension, plant life in general, must possess a degree of sentience.

At the macro scale, the world (as revealed by our unaided senses), life forms are characterized by growth, in the sense of growing bigger, from their birth in the seed. This is a characteristic that plants and animals have in common. But living things do not merely grow bigger, they develop in different configurations also. The caterpillar that becomes a butterfly is only one example of developmental change that occurs, if less dramatically, in organic growth processes of all kinds.

The manner of this growth cannot be entirely pre-determined. An individual life form must to a certain extent innovate in response to new conditions in its environment. Particularly this is the case with its own kind. Each generation is a slightly different version of its parents, not a carbon copy. The existentialists noted this fact in human beings. By Darwin's law it must be true also, *to a degree,* for all life forms.

Organicity

The theory of Experientialism, described above, is the only scientifically respectable account of the origin of life there is. It states that the potential for some kind of life is present in all kinds of matter. The smallest unit of matter manifests as a particle and, at the same time, a wave.

As a wave, it is a growth impulse, a pulsation of pre-conscious desire. As a particle, we define it as a unit of identity.

But in the real world (outside the scientists' laboratories) this fundamental particle always exists in combination with others, as an atom. An atom is already a *community* of sub-atomic particles, an organized community, an organism.

A particle, such as an electron, is a point. It has no extension, no interior and therefore no exterior, it is a mere pulsation of desire. It is merely a 'wanting' to grow.

Growth at the elemental level, is achieved by combination. Several sub-atomic particles combine to form an atom. Atoms combine to form a molecule. But a molecule has a growth impulse equal to the combined strength of the atoms that compose it.

So, when conditions allow, two hydrogen atoms may form a love triangle with an oxygen atom and form water. These water molecules have a growth impulse to add themselves to others of their own kind by simple *addition*. We are now at the scale where the naked eye can observe a drop of water reaching out to another drop. When they touch, they fall at once into a full embrace and do what they want to do, which is to grow into a larger drop.

There are other atoms forming other kinds of combination, which float in the environment provided by 'bodies' of water. These eventually combine again in such a way as to form bio-chemicals. At a certain point there develop combinations that achieve a fundamentally new way to process their compounded growth impulses. This is what the ancients called 'autopoiesis.'[41]

Organisms grow themselves by symbiotic interaction of the myriad organs, organelles and micro-organisms that compose them. At this scale, and all higher scales, growth is achieved by *multiplication*, so to speak, whereas at the micro scale it can only be by addition.

But macro-organisms, that is to say, plants and animals (including humans), although self-regulated, do not cease to grow by addition after they have achieved the capacity to grow by multiplication. They all do this naturally, by forming communities of their own kind, organically related as colonies, hives, families, tribes, nations, and associations of all kinds.

Combinations of individual entities that interact in such a way as to form larger entities are called compound entities. But most of the universe is composed of aggregations of individual entities that do not interact in such a way. These are called aggregates, or in popular parlance, 'inert.'

The world is self-creating through the agency of its organisms

We give to this phenomenon, which grows out of A. N. Whitehead's scientifically sanctioned view of the world, the name Organicity.

What went wrong?

We mistook the world for something apart from ourselves, instead of understanding ourselves as a part of the natural order. Humans exist as a result of a chance mutation. We are as we are, but we might have been different.

We have banged away at the non-human world, trying to shape it to our own advantage, like a blacksmith beating an iron bar into a blade. But we are sawing off the branch we are standing on, like a mad carpenter.

What is this branch? It is the eco-system, an intricate web of connections between all life forms and the physical environment which sustains them.

It is the tragedy of the modern world that the West inherited a religious tradition of human exclusivity that fostered the illusion we could do what we like with nature, which was seen as not including us. This left us free to pursue instrumental reason, solely in the interests of our own species, ignoring the interests of others. In fact, we acted as if no other entities in the universe besides ourselves could possibly have interests of any comparable kind.

And we succeeded brilliantly at making life more comfortable for ourselves and increasing our life expectancy. We did not notice, or pretended not to notice, that this was all at the expense of other life forms, who suffered, and continue to suffer as a consequence. This illusory independence fostered the economic system that has now become globalised.

Meanwhile, the religious traditions of the East, which preached a much more accurate account of the life system of which we are a part, have become largely marginalized. However, the East never produced what the West, and now the whole world, regards as 'progress.'

But as Peter Singer remarked, *'we are quite literally gambling with the future of our planet—for the sake of hamburgers.'*

Science begat technology. Technology yielded many benefits for humanity. But we now know it has a hugely dangerous side effect, global warming.

Does this mean science is a bad thing? No. On the contrary, we need more science, not less. Had we known enough about the side effects, we would never have transformed our entire global productive and transportation systems to fossil fueled technologies.

Now we are locked in. Huge investments have been made in an infrastructure we now know needs to be rapidly dismantled and replaced. So why don't 'we' act on that knowledge?

The climate scientists know well enough what needs to be done. They are shouting at us. STOP BURNING FOSSIL FUELS!

Everyone hears the command except those who have the power to impose obedience to it. Oxfam recently calculated that just eight individuals now have the same wealth as the poorest half of the global population. An economic system so immensely profitable to the few who own its commanding heights, is extremely hard to change, especially in a few years.

We need a *peaceful* revolution. The world has never witnessed such a thing. But anthropogenic global warming is also unprecedented. Therefore, historical precedent is no longer a useful guide. Equally unprecedented is the mine of information now available to all and sundry. Previous revolutions have often failed because their leaders lied to the masses for selfish reasons. Today this is much harder to do.

Necessary course corrections

We should come to our senses and start behaving rationally:

- Warfare, as institutionalized mass murder, is NOT rational.
- The military/industrial complex that promotes warfare, is NOT rational.
- Continuing to produce GHG's beyond the capacity of natural carbon sinks to absorb it, is NOT rational.
- An economic system which perpetually robs the poor and powerless to further enrich the already rich and powerful, is NOT rational.
- To submit to market forces blindly is NOT rational.
- But to pay no heed to market forces, when they indicate a sudden fall in prices for renewable energy systems, below the costs of existing fossil fuel-based systems, is also NOT rational.
- Above all, denying a threat to survival, especially when the means of removing it are known and available, is NOT rational.

Empathy and Compassion

But, in the long run, cold reason is not enough. Unless our species cultivates more consciously its innate sense of connection with other life forms, we may not survive.

Our growing awareness of likeness with other animals should engender a new sense of our moral responsibility to consider their interests as well as our own.

The head and the heart must come to know each other again. Eros meet Logos. You two have been too long estranged.

David Dobereiner – 17.01.17

Notes

[37] *I am indebted here to the arguments of Max Stirner in The Ego and its Own.*

[38] *It is almost unbelievable that Descartes, who is said to have owned and loved his pet dog, could have seen nothing in it but a machine.*

[39] *'Any doctrine which refuses to place human experience outside nature, must find in descriptions of human experience factors which also enter into the descriptions of less specialized natural occurrences. If there be no such factors, then the doctrine of human experience as a fact within nature is mere bluff ... we should either admit dualism ... or we should point out the identical elements connecting human experience with physical science' – A. N. Whitehead*

[40] *'The opposition of the real and the idea(l) is an irreconcilable one, and the one can never become the other: if the ideal become the real, it would no longer be the ideal, and if the real become the ideal, the ideal alone would be, but not at all the real', 'No idea has existence, for none is capable of corporeity' – Max Stirner*

[41] *A term borrowed by Fritjof Capra and Luisi in their book 'A Systems View of Life.'*

CHAPTER 12

CORE PRINCIPLES OF ORGANICITY

1. Nature is all there is.
2. A fundamental attribute of life is self-optimization.
3. The distinction between humans and animals is a false one. Humans are animals.
4. There appear to be two opposed impulses embedded in nature: Evolution and Entropy.
5. Will Evolution OR Entropy finally triumph? In fact, there will be no end, because nature, time, space, movement, change and diversity are all infinite, with no beginning and no end.
6. Each birth is a new creation.
7. Nature never repeats itself precisely. Perfection is a myth, or rather the perfection of nature lies only in its infinite diversity.
8. Predominantly, males and females search for the most attractive member of the other and reach the height of happiness and well-being in the pleasure and joy, that only they can bring to each other.
9. Machines are reproduced. Organisms recreate, or more accurately, procreate.
10. Modernity has diverted the natural human desire to please and be pleased by contact or association

with other humans or other beings, into a lust for the possession of manufactured objects.

11. This diversion of energies into the acquisition of material objects has had the cumulative effect of cutting us off from each other as well as from our fellow animals, and plants with whom we evolved.

12. In our efforts to build robots more and more like ourselves we have not noticed how robotic we ourselves have become. With disastrous results.

Dear David

Hi!

Most of that looks to me pretty sensible and uncontroversial—
though, of course, people can always start a controversy about the
definition of terms.

Do you want to raise a controversy about some part of it?

all the best

yours,

Mary Midgley.

EPILOGUE AND
ACKNOWLEDGEMENTS

I am writing this epilogue a year or so after the bulk of the book was finished enough to send to the publisher. Much has happened in the world during this interval that reinforces the urgency of its message.

My main intent was to sound the alarm, as loudly as I could, so that the necessary switch to renewable energy and a plant-based diet, can be accomplished *soon enough* to save our planet from the heat death we humans are causing, before it becomes too late.

The latest news from the climate scientists is that this deadline for completion of the revolutionary transformation of everything we do and how we do it, has moved closer and closer. To complete net carbon neutrality, humanity does not have a hundred years, nor even fifty, but *twelve years,* starting from 2018. Otherwise global warming will exceed the 1.5° above pre-industrial levels, now recognized as the safe limit.

The news of this existential crisis is at last getting through to the general public, (mostly via the Internet) in spite of the efforts of the mainstream media to conceal it (because it's not good for ratings). Hence, in recent days we have seen groups of citizens self-organizing to form groups such as Extinction Rebellion. At the time of writing, over a thousand members of this group temporarily blocked the Thames bridges in central London. This significant coordinated act of non-violent civil disobedience was barely mentioned in the UK mainstream media.

So, in one sense, the book's central purpose, sounding the alarm, has been picked up by others and is now 'joining the chorus.'

But, of course, the book does much more than that. It looks beyond the revolution, now hopefully just beginning on the bridges of London, and asks a number of questions: What comes after the revolution? What will prevent it going bad, like most previous revolutions? How did we get into this predicament in the first place, when we thought we were behaving so rationally?

This last question is crucial. If we try to solve the present crisis from the same anthropocentric position that brought us the Industrial Revolution we will probably fail again, in some other equally unforeseen way. We must eschew the anthropocentric and embrace the biocentric if we are ever to achieve the kind of harmonious eco-system that includes all earthly life, not just the human, in what Kropotkin called a 'fugitive equilibrium' and I call Organicity.

Imagine a world where the cars, trucks, buses, ships and planes will no longer exist in the form we see most of them today. The plastic products, which are ubiquitous, will be gone too, because they are a cheap bi-product of the fossil fuel industry, which itself can no longer be permitted to exist.

The *technical* means for achieving this transformation are known and have been analysed by several authors. The problem is *political.*

In the words of George Monbiot:

> *Because we cannot save ourselves without contesting oligarchic control, the fight for democracy and justice and the fight against environmental breakdown are one and the same. Do not allow those who have caused this crisis to define the limits of political action. Do not allow those whose magical thinking got us into this mess to tell us what can and cannot be done.*

But contesting oligarchic control is not the same as questioning the need for oligarchies in the first place. There are two poles to political philosophy, Oligarchy, or the rule of some kind of elite group of individuals over the masses, is one pole.

The other pole is Anarchy, meaning, literally, *no* rule. This, in practice, defaults to *self*-rule, or rather the filtering of the will of individuals through direct democratic participation in weekly assembly of all members of each and every community.

Why history is replete with examples of nations and empires favoring the former tendency and so rare is it to find examples of the latter is an interesting question, which I attempt to address in the earlier chapters of this book. The reason it is important is that, if there is some tendency that has biased our social evolution in a predominantly authoritarian direction, that makes us seek power to control the other to our own exclusive advantage, then, before we can advance the Extinction Rebellion, we need to become consciously aware of this bias so that we can consciously correct it.

Otherwise we will repeat the same mistake of replacing one Oligarch with another; Tsar Nicholas with Stalin.

Otherwise we may not succeed in replacing the false doctrine of Neo-Darwinism with that which this great scientist actually observed. This was more often 'Mutual Aid' than 'Survival of the Fittest.' Genes that survive best in nature are those that belong to individuals who reproduce best, and these are usually those most attractive to the opposite sex.

❧

My later life transition from 'ecotecture' to political philosophy is partly explained by this insight. Environment, conceived as something separate from humanity is a false and misleading concept. The primary aspect of environment for any social animal, is the social environment. This social environment is framed by a set of assumptions that are shared (often unconsciously) by members of each human society.

These assumptions may be exposed and questioned in some philosophical discussion groups, but are rarely discussed in political party meetings.

For example, the neo-liberal doctrine that 'free markets can solve all problems' has blinded those currently in charge to the obvious fact about the world's worst problems. Some of these are, in no particular order, inequality, climate breakdown, poverty, obesity related health problems, mass extinctions, desertification, wealth distribution etc. They are all an inevitable by-product of an economic system based on endless growth and capital accumulation, which is its raison d'etre.

✎

As I approach my ninetieth year, and complete the final pages of what will surely be my last book, I feel the need to acknowledge and thank those family members, teachers, mentors and authors, who have helped me throughout my career (even though many of these are no longer living). They not only helped me navigate my way through professional institutions, but, in so doing, shaped my character and to some extent made me what I am.

This will be not so much an autobiography, as a history of the development of the concept of Organicity, traced through my personal interaction with those who significantly influenced it. This is itself an example of the organic growth of an idea in the soil of its life-long immersion in a changing social environment.

MY MOTHER, DOROTHY
DOBEREINER (NÉE HASSALL)

I loved my mother more than most because from the age of 4 she was the only parent present in our home. I was her fifth child, born 2 months overdue, with difficulty, in 1929. My family lived mostly on welfare, in a series of rural cottages in the Berkshire Downs above Blewbury.

My siblings were mostly away from home and the one closest to me in age, my brother Peter, was still 4 years older than me. So, most of the time, when I was not at school in the village, I felt as if I was the only human in a natural world stretching to the horizon in all directions. I came to know rooks and skylarks better than other kids. I learned to play alone. This must have prepared me to see other organisms as subject beings like myself.

I think I also learned something about the virtues of frugality. My earliest memories are of living in a house with no plumbing and no electricity. There was a sink in the kitchen but it had no taps. Water came from a well just in front of the garden fence. You could pull the big bucket up from the deep well by its long rope if you were strong enough. The privy was in the back garden with its own slightly smaller bucket. There was one fireplace and one paraffin lamp. In winter you went to bed with a candle.

Later my mother managed to send my sister, Omy, to the same boarding school she had attended herself (no doubt courtesy of a wealthy aunt). Then, by working as the cook in a posh Prep. School in the New Forest she managed to start Peter and me off on the road to Oxbridge, while she herself lived in a caravan on the school grounds.

Later, after the war began, my mother's circumstances greatly improved, when my father returned to service as a Major in the Canadian army, and there was an automatic 'spouse allowance.' She had never divorced him. She had simply taken herself and her five kids and moved to another continent.

My mother then managed to send me to what was then a 'public' school, Magdalen College School in Oxford. This experience changed my life through the agency of:

PETER GREENHAM

Peter Greenham had a job as my English teacher at Magdalen College School. But he was a really fine academic painter and later became, the Keeper of the Royal Academy.

Greenham knew about my aunt, Joan Hassall OBE, who had attended the same art school, the Byam Shaw School of Art. He also knew about my family's other three celebrities, my mother's father, John Hassall, my Uncle Christopher and my cousin, Imogen Hassall.

So Greenham took upon himself to give me private drawing and painting lessons. Thus my 'career' started while still at school. I became proficient enough as a painter to have three of my paintings exhibited in the annual Young Contemporaries Exhibition, a selection of the best student works from UK art schools.

Greenham became a sort of surrogate father to me. He had assumed that since he had trained me as a painter, I would follow him into the world of fine arts. I explained to him my reservations about painting pictures as a career for myself. I wondered whether I could make a living at it and, even if I did manage to do that, in what way would I be 'making the world a better place?' I felt that a professional must provide a service to society. This was primary. Self-gratification was a secondary consideration. Besides, I wasn't just good at art. I was equally gifted at mathematics, solid geometry in particular.

Greenham, thought about this and came back with his advice. 'You should become an architect,' he said. 'What is an architect?' I asked. 'Architecture has been characterized as the Mother of all the Arts' he replied.

So, the same person who taught me how to paint, also launched me on my main career as an architect. He advised and assisted me to enter the Architectural Association School of Architecture.

Greenham also taught me to admire the writings of D. H. Lawrence. I read many of DHL's works and they greatly influenced me in developing a respect for, and even a reverence for, the will to live, in humans and other animals. This favouring of the Organic over the Machinic was to stay with me for life and was to flower in my concept of Organicity. Since DHL was an apostle of Nietzsche (so critics say), his influence formed a bridge to my third 'career,' Philosophy, which is perhaps the best way of describing what I have been doing since retiring from the practice and teaching of architecture and urbanism.

I have no academic credentials in philosophy so the theory of Organicity grew out of my own reflections on the books I was reading and the conversations from other groups in the Newcastle Philosophy Society. I dipped into the classical authors, Plato, Aristotle, Nietzsche, Hegel, the French post modernists, Kropotkin, Wittgenstein, and A. N. Whitehead. I have a particular bone to pick with Descartes, which I dealt with in my first book, already mentioned.

But the most profound influences, in my experience, are those where readings are augmented by at least one private conversation with the author. I was privileged to have had this opportunity with Frank Lloyd Wright, Murray Bookchin, Noam Chomsky, Fritjof Capra, and Mary Midgley.

D. H. LAWRENCE

People who knew DHL often remarked on his unique ability to see into the very soul of a person or an animal, and then express their essence in poetic language. Even Bertrand Russell, who at one time was a friend of his, granted him this incredible gift.

As a teenager, when I first read Sons and Lovers, I was excited by the close fit between the emotional tone of the book and the natural teenager feelings that were going on inside myself at the time.

He wrote most convincingly of the motivation and conduct of other animals like dogs, chipmunks, snakes and cats, as if he knew somehow what it would be like to be one such.

When I later came to consider Darwin's statement that 'humans differ from other animals in degree but not kind,' I was more than ready to accept it, and to draw far reaching conclusions from it. DHL had prepared the ground for me.

A quotation from one of Lawrence's essays became my credo:

We know that the rose comes to blossom. We know that we are incipient with blossom. It is our business to go as we are impelled, with faith, and pure spontaneous morality, knowing that the rose blossoms and taking that knowledge for sufficient.

Flowers are the plant equivalent of the sexual organs of an animal, since 'mating' and reproduction is carried out by insect pollinators passing from one plant to another through their blossoms.

DHL implies that when a rose blossom's, it is having the plant equivalent of an orgasm. If we have 'faith and pure spontaneous morality,' we will recognize our strongest human desires are telling us what we *should* do, just as the rose knows what it *must* do.

Because we are much more complex beings, we experience multiple desires pulling us in all sorts of different directions. When sexual desire is felt, and communicated *mutually*, that is to say, when two individuals feel equally strong attraction for each other, the effect can be overpowering to both parties. It is rightly described as '*falling* in love.'

PATRICK HORSBRUGH

Patrick was my first employer after I finished my architectural training. He had earned his diploma at the AA a few years ahead of me. While I was in my fifth and final year at the same institution, I came across a very interesting model of an urban design project that must have been the final thesis of some former student.

The reason it interested me was that it was designed on a hexagonal grid, not the usual Cartesian square grid. Now, the one consistent feature of my own work as a student was that none of them conformed to the dictates of a square grid. My admiration for Frank Lloyd Wright's work had made me see that to arrive at the Organic the 'right' angle is often the wrong angle. Organisms take many forms but none of them are box shaped. Organisms may move in a straight line but any change of direction must be mediated by a curve. Streets laid out on a hexagonal grid would obviate the need for traffic lights. Roads would never cross.

I found out the name of the creator of the model and immediately went for an interview. It was Patrick Horsbrugh. Needless to say, we found we had much in common, including an admiration for the work of FLW and his concept of Organic Architecture.

Where we differed was in our family background. Patrick was a well-connected member of the Scottish aristocracy. I was, by comparison, a nobody.

The project the office was working on was to develop a 40-acre bomb site in the center of London. It was called the New Barbican. It was understood that Patrick's connections could possibly ensure that the project, once finished, and approved by the authorities, might stand a good chance of actually being built.

Like the model I had seen at the AA it consisted of three main elements. There was a Podium, consisting of a single 3,4 or 5 story blocks of mixed commercial uses, including parking and loading docks for trucks, covering the whole site. On top of the Podium, around its edges, were sited high rise buildings, containing offices and housing. The roof of the Podium then became the 'agora,' a traffic free public space with shopping, pubs, cafes and clubs in the base of the towers.

It is only now, in retrospect, I realize how much working on this project must have inspired me. Sixty years ago, I worked on the New Barbican, a superblock enabled by German bombers in the center of London.

For the last ten years I have been looking at a framed, computer drawn, project of mine, called New Braintree. It shows a whole city transformed into superblocks. Each block is a different shaped and sized free formed polygon whose corners never coincide in numbers greater than three. The roads that follow the edges of the blocks therefore never cross. These roads also never encounter pedestrians. Their pathways are on higher levels.

The form of the superblock in my work is, however, radically different from Patrick's. In my case the 'podium' is no longer a solid block, with a commons space on its roof, but hollowed out, to form a living amphitheater, with its commons on the ground in the center. My concept of an Eco-city has no high-rise buildings, because they imply a class hierarchy, which will no longer exist in Matripolis. Even if towers were designed as social housing, they would not succeed. They would inevitably increase the social alienation already running rampant in the present market-based system of mature capitalism.

∽

Patrick was always a good friend of mine. He was my first employer in London, in 1955. In 1958 he phoned me from USA where he was teaching at Dept. of Architecture, University of Illinois, Urbana. He said the head of the graduate school would be visiting Europe and would like to interview me for a teaching job at the Urbana campus.

Thus, Patrick's recommendation lead to my moving to USA with my wife and child, and embarking on a career of teaching architectural design in US and Canadian universities for most of the rest of my life.

Patrick had promised Winston Churchill, on his death bed, that he would see to the construction of a memorial building in USA. He arranged an interview with Frank Lloyd Wright, and asked me if I would like to come along (with a roll of my drawings). FLW never got the commission to build a Churchill memorial (he raised impossible conditions) and I never got enrolled as a Wright apprentice (he said I was too late, he was too old). As the interview ended, Wright walked us to the door past a portrait of his mother. He remarked, as we did so, 'that was my mother. She made me an architect.' Wright died later that same year.

About 2008 Patrick told me about the RSA. He recommended me as a Fellow.

I was accepted and Patrick paid for my first year's subscription.

I returned to UK later that year and have been attending the local meetings of that august institution in Newcastle ever since.

KARL LINN

Karl Linn was a fully qualified psychoanalyst and landscape architect. He used these qualifications in the service of advancing social change—as an activist, an extremely successful one. The record of his innovative projects is enshrined in the book he wrote that was published posthumously, with the help of some of his disciples, of whom I was one. The name of his book is *Building Commons and Community*. The first two words of this title are meant literally and metaphorically. The last word should be read literally—but as a result of the Commons building process.

Karl practiced a highly innovative and original form of landscape architectural education. Whichever campus he visited he would first do a survey of the slums that lay closest to the campus. Then he would take his students out of their design studio to meet the people living in the slum. The students would hear the needs of the residents; ranging from sand pits for the younger children, swings, and basketball facilities for older children, perhaps a duck pond, pleasant seating areas for older adults, etc.

The students would then be led by Karl to find a suitable vacant site near the center of the neighborhood, and after all the necessary arrangements with local authorities and charities had been made, the students *and* local volunteers, would build a Neighborhood Commons, under Karl's leadership.

Karl's idea was that this common space, if properly designed and built, would make it possible for the residents to meet each other, and form a real community, like an extended family. There would be community gardens where mothers and/or unemployed parents could work to provide food for their families while their children played nearby. But most importantly, there would always be a place of assembly—seats arranged in a rough circle with a surface in the middle hard enough to dance on.

Karl always made sure that the residents would need to form a permanent committee to govern the maintenance and use of the commons. It was *their* space and no outside officials would have anything to do with it.

Once, I asked Karl if he was an anarchist, like me. No, he replied. But I never met or heard of anyone, in academia or anywhere else, who more closely followed anarchist principles in his work, life, or teachings.

For over 40 years Karl was my best friend, mentor, enabler, associate, and employer. When I left teaching at the Rhode Island School of Design he told me about a job opening at the Massachusetts College of Art, the only state supported art college in USA. They had approached Karl, who was then teaching at MIT, to start an Architectural Design department at MassArt. The idea was that poorer students could get on a 'career ladder,' doing a three-year course at an art school, which would then allow them to enter a Master's degree program in Architecture at MIT or Harvard.

Karl had accepted the assignment, but he needed me to write the architectural curriculum and assemble a faculty to teach the courses. There was already a Design Division at the college, but no architectural design department.

Later Karl tried to get me to join him on the MIT faculty. He persuaded Kevin Lynch to allow me to lecture to his class. Afterwards, he told Karl that my lecture was good, but I could not be employed at MIT without a master's degree, which at that time I did not have.

Karl recommended me to head the architecture department at MassArt after he left. Thus, I became a department head for a few years until I came up for tenure.

Towards the end of his life Karl employed me, full time, to assist him with the graphics of his book. I owe him a lot. He was a great man.

MURRAY BOOKCHIN

It must have been in the early 70's that I drove from Boston to Washington DC to join a Vietnam war protest march. I naturally carried my black flag over to where the other anarchists were displaying theirs. After the march, I gave a ride back to Boston for one of them.

I thus became involved for the first time in organized anarchist activities and soon learned about the central importance of Murray Bookchin and Noam Chomsky. I helped form the Cambridge-based Black Rose Collective and used my graphic design skills to produce what was supposed to become a monthly publication. It was called Black Rose Magazine: A Journal of Contemporary Anarchism.

Murray used to come down from Burlington, Vermont to take part in the demos in Boston. I met him on one of these occasions and a couple of times he chose to stay over in my commune rather than one of the hard-core anarchist ones that were also available.

Towards the end of his life, Murray had by his bedside a pre-publication draft of my book, 'The End of the Street.' It's a pity he never lived to read it because it is the only presentation of an urban design system intended to accommodate citizens living according to Murray's principles of Libertarian Municipalism.

Stated another way, my earlier book presents a future post-revolutionary ecocity that would address equally, the requirements of *natural* ecology with Murray's *social* ecology. No other architect/urbanist/author has done that as far as I know. (This was my reply to Janet Biehl's question).

Murray's political philosophy evolved from communism to Trotskyite to social anarchist to communalism to municipalism.

My own development was different. Since I started as an architect, I naturally started with the built form of an ecocity.

That was Matripolis, or Organi-City. *This* book expands the political philosophy into a philosophy of life in general. Organicity does not deal with the far future ideal city but with the immediate existential crisis of climate breakdown that a social and economic system based on hierarchal divisions of human society has caused.

But both books are deeply indebted to the thought and teachings of the great Murray Bookchin.

NOAM CHOMSKY

When I first moved to the Boston area in the early 70's, I was accepted by a group of MIT graduate students who were looking for one other member to form a commune. We all moved into a flat in Somerville, and that is where I learned about the theories of Noam Chomsky, the person who had formed and headed the Linguistics Department where they spent their working days.

I remember the first subject of conversation was Chomsky's observation that very young children, as soon as they had learned to speak, could utter a sentence that was completely original. It could be something that had never before been said.

Did this demonstrate that humans have free will? Did it show that Behavourism theory was rubbish?

❧

It was through the Black Rose Collective that I first came face to face with Noam. I had been engaged with the Collective in producing the BR Journal. Since I was the only one with graphic design skills, I designed the cover and contributed some illustrations. I also wrote an article, Anarchist Planning, for Black Rose 1.

It was decided we should request an interview with Noam that would be recorded and published in the same first issue of our Journal. It was at this interview that I was able to meet and discuss issues with the internationally famed public intellectual, for the first time.

Our collective also took part in another discussion. We decided it would be fruitful to arrange a discussion between Noam Chomsky and Murray Bookchin. Each of these anarchist theorists knew of each other but had never actually met.

The first interview was published and is freely available, to this day, on the Internet, but the second one, as far as I know, was never recorded. This is regrettable as the differences between these two, though subtle, would have been very interesting, and my aging memory leaves me certain that the meeting happened, and that I was there. But of what was said, I remember not a word.

Years later, I came up for tenure at the institution where I was Head of the Department of Architectural Design. My fellow communards strongly urged me to ask Noam Chomsky for a letter of recommendation to the tenure committee. I protested that I hardly knew him and he knew nothing about my work. They said don't worry, he will do it for you and he will do it very well.

Figure 2 shows the resulting letter:

DEPARTMENT OF FOREIGN LITERATURES
AND LINGUISTICS

MASSACHUSETTS INSTITUTE OF TECHNOLOGY

CAMBRIDGE, MASSACHUSETTS 02139

3 March 1975

Dr. John W. Cataldo
Dean of Academic Affairs
Mass. College of Art
364 Brookline Avenue
Boston, MA 02115

Dear Dean Cataldo,

I understand that David Dobereiner is being considered for a tenured
position at the College. I hope that it will not be out of place if
I write some unsolicited comments on his behalf. I do not, in fact,
know Mr. Dobereiner very well, but have met him several times and had
some lengthy and interesting discussions with him about questions of
culture, politics and society. I have also read an article of his
entitled "Anarchist planning," which dealt with topics that have long
been of great interest to me. I found him to be a thoughtful critic,
with a grasp of serious problems and a willingness to devote hard
thinking to them. Parts of our discussion were carried in the issue
of Black Rose in which his article appears; what value it may have
derives in considerable measure from his penetrating comments and
suggestions, which I found extremely valuable. On the basis of these
contacts, I formed a very high impression of his ability, intellectual
integrity and commitment. I am not competent to comment on his professional work, and am indeed unacquainted with it, but he is a person
whom I would personally very much like to have as a colleague.

Sincerely yours,

Noam Chomsky

NC: fak

Figure 2

My 2015 argument with Noam

Many moons ago I participated in an Internet chat group with Noam Chomsky, Michael Albert, and two others.

They were all standing on a purely humanist/Enlightenment platform that says, roughly, the human mind is unique in the universe with no comparison to anything else.

Animals are machines, and the human body is itself a machine.

I was arguing the opposite. Humans are organisms that have evolved from other organisms and all organisms differ from each other 'in degree but not kind' (Darwin). There must be some degree of cognition therefore, in any creature that moves around.

So, it was with great interest that I read the lecture.[42] It was given by Noam (at the Vatican !?) and recently published on the Internet.

I could almost flatter myself that my argument had influenced him because his present position is much closer to mine now than it was when we chatted.

He now says, for instance, Cartesian dualism was good science in the 17th Century but '… *like much normal science it was soon shown to be incorrect.*'

Further on he says '… *Charles Darwin … wrote that there is no need to regard thought, 'a secretion of the brain' as 'more wonderful than gravity, a property of matter'—all inconceivable to us, but that is not a fact about the external world; rather, about our cognitive limitations.*'

Now I agree with that, except for a minor quibble about the use of the word 'secretion' and also, in fact, I oppose the received opinion that consciousness is all in the brain. I believe it permeates the whole environment contained in the membrane sack of the skin, and quite possibly radiates even beyond that.

For Chomsky, Cartesian dualism was disproved by Newton '… *who exorcised the machine, leaving the ghost intact, contrary to what is commonly believed.*' He points to the findings of modern biology and asserts that humans

> *... will be like all other organisms in having a genetic endowment that enables them to grow and develop to their mature form. By simple logic, the endowment that makes this possible also excludes other paths of development.* The endowment that yields scope also establishes limits. *What enables us to grow legs and arms, and a mammalian visual system, prevents us from growing wings and having an insect visual system.*

He goes on to develop this idea of natural limits to human understanding, which to my mind is a post-humanist notion, but which Chomsky attributes to the Enlightenment itself. Since the sub-title of my first book is '*Sustainable Growth within Natural Limits,*' I am obviously sympathetic, but a bit surprised to find it coming from a mind that has always rigorously adhered to rules of the scientific method. Was it Leonardo or some other giant of Italian Renaissance who uttered the exaltation 'Man can do anything if he will!'? Yet NC insists that later '*... great figures in the scientific revolution and the Enlightenment believed that there are phenomena that fall beyond human understanding.*'

There is an interesting distinction between the concepts of infinite and limitless. '*...infinite ... is not the same as limitless. English is infinite, but doesn't include Greek.*'

I quote the last paragraph in the lecture in full because it focuses precisely on the argument that ensued in the chat that took place some twenty years ago.

> *Honesty should lead us to concede, I think, that we understand little more today about these matters than the Spanish physician-philosopher Juan Huarte did 500 years ago when he distinguished the kind of intelligence humans shared with animals from the higher grade that humans alone possess and is illustrated in the creative use of language, and proceeding beyond that, from the still higher grade illustrated in true artistic*

and scientific creativity. Nor do we even know whether these are questions that lie within the scope of human understanding, or whether they fall among what Hume took to be Nature's ultimate secrets, consigned to 'that obscurity in which they ever did and ever will remain.

I argued then, and still do, that the implication that our 'higher grades' of human creativity puts us in some exclusive category (harking back to the Biblical assertion that 'God made man in his image')—this is false.

There is overwhelming evidence that other species communicate with each other non-linguistically, must engage in some form of image-based thought analogous to the human, and are creative, playful, loving, curious and inventive at times.

They are not lesser, and we are not superior. Each species inhabits a different world according to the scope and limits of its genetic endowment. This does not mean the different species don't or can't interact with each other. They do, all the time.

There are indeed things we will never be able to understand, like the navigational achievements of migrating birds, any more than a bird will ever be able to appreciate a Rembrandt portrait.

Without going all the way with Arne Naess's assertion that every species has *intrinsic* value (but where do we draw the line?), we nevertheless should be vitally concerned that modern industrial society is causing the sixth mass extinction since life on earth began.

We have followed the Biblical injunction to 'be fruitful and multiply' faithfully, but at the expense of other life forms, except for those we have found we can exploit for our own use.

We have brought on ourselves the climate crisis—our moment of truth.

Can we now rapidly re-discover our connection with the Earth and its non-human inhabitants, with whom we share the same needs? In doing so, we might find it useful to reflect that our *higher* achievements may have had a downside. In being *higher,* they have taken us further from the earth, the soil from which we are sprung.

Can we get back down to earth in time to save it from the heat build-up our GHG emissions are causing?

Time (the next 15 years) will tell.

Notes

42   *http://www.informationclearinghouse.info/article40996.htm*

FRITJOF CAPRA

It must have been about 1988, or thereabouts, that I met Fritjof Capra. I was living alone in Berkeley California at the time. Charlotte Hardman, who knew Fritjof, was visiting me at the time. She had assumed we would be interested in meeting each other, and had arranged for Fritjof to come to tea with us in my apartment.

He drove up and parked in the common driveway. His was an impressive vintage car that looked as if it might have been a Bentley Roadster or some such.

It must have been at least 15 years later that I read *The Systems View of Life* by Capra and Luisi. This was during the time when I was running the monthly meetings for the Newcastle Philosophy Society that provided all the material for *this* book, Organicity.

When I went back to my copy of the book, I got a shock. There were more underlined passages than I have ever seen in *any* book. I thought, at first, that the book must have had far more of an influence on my development of the concept of Organicity than I had ever admitted to myself.

On further reflection, I realized that the evidence of my excitement on reading *The Systems View* was not because it informed me of something new but because it confirmed what I was already 'teaching' my 'class.'

Nevertheless, the later chapters must have influenced me and, therefore, I do have to concede that I must acknowledge Capra and Luisi as being hugely important in my work, arguably, more so than any other authors.

Since this last section of the book is an Epilogue, I must assume the reader will have already read the preceding text. The most honest way for me to demonstrate my debt to Capra and Luisi is to quote from their book directly.

I will therefore quote, for the last pages of mine, most of the underlined passages, page by page, from theirs. This will allow the reader to feel the resonance with my own words:

> *p 8 Cartesian mechanism was expressed in the dogma that the laws of biology can ultimately be reduced to those of physics and chemistry.*

> *p 10 ... the next wave of opposition to the mechanistic conception of life, the school known as organismic biology, or 'organicism.'*

> *According to the systems view, an organism, or living system, is an integrated whole whose essential properties cannot be reduced to those of its parts.*

> *p 13 These two tendencies—the self-assertive and the integrative—are both essential aspects of all living systems ... Neither of them is intrinsically good or bad. What is good, or healthy, is a dynamic balance; what is bad, or unhealthy, is inbalance—overemphasis on one tendency and neglect of the other.*

> *p 14 It (Deep Ecology) is a world view that acknowledges the* inherent value of nonhuman life, *recognizing that all living beings are members of ecological communities, bound together in networks of interdependencies. When this deep ecological perception becomes part of our daily awareness, a radically new system of ethics emerges.*

> *p 15 The paradigm shift in science, at its deepest level, involves a perceptual shift from physics to the life sciences.*

p 56 ... the continuing illusion of unlimited growth on a finite planet is the fundamental dilemma at the roots of all the major problems of our time. It is the result of a clash between linear, reductionist thinking and the non-linear patterns in our biosphere—the ecological networks and cycles that constitute the web of life'.

p 132 Living things ... what is their common denominator? ... self-maintenance via a mechanism of self-regeneration from within ...

... life is not localized: life is a global property, arising from the collective interactions of the molecular species within the cell.

p 133 The properties of life are emergent properties which cannot be reduced to the properties of the components.

p 134 ... the living being needs nutrients and energy, and these acquisitions are parts of its own life.

p 135 ... the living organism is an operationally closed system with a circular logic.

p 136 ... the behaviour of a living organism is determined. However, rather than being determined by outside forces, it is determined by the organism's own structure—a structure formed by a succession of autonomous structural changes. Hence, the behaviour of the living organism is both determined, and free.

p 142 Mind is always present in a bodily structure: and, vice versa, a truly living organism must be capable of cognition (the process of knowing).

p 160 Emergence is one of the hallmarks of life. It has been recognized as the dynamic origin of development, learning, and evolution. In other words, creativity—the generation of new forms—is a key property of all living systems. And since emergence is an integral part of the dynamics of open systems, open systems develop and evolve. Life constantly reaches out into novelty.

p 180 In static systems, self-organization, and the resulting emergent properties are relatively simple concepts, well explained by chemistry and physics, but in dynamic systems the processes of self-organization, and emergence, are subtle and complex, and their outcomes are often unforeseeable, both in biological and in social life.

p 253 ... mind is the essence of being alive.

p 254 Mind—or more accurately, mental activity is immanent in matter at all levels of life.

Living systems are cognitive systems, and living as a process is a process of cognition. This statement is valid for all organisms, with and without a nervous system (Maturana).

p 255 Maturana ... sees no essential difference between the process of human cognition and the cognitive processes of other living beings.

p 256 ... to live is to know. Describing cognition as the breath of life seems to be a perfect metaphor.

p 257 The entire structure of the organism participates in the process of cognition, whether or not the organism has a brain and a higher nervous system ... At all levels of life, beginning with the simplest cell, mind and matter, process and structure, are inseparably connected. For the first time, we have a scientific theory that unifies mind, matter and life.

p 261 A full understanding of biological phenomena is reached only when we approach it through the interplay of three different levels of description—the biology of the observed phenomena, the laws of physics and biochemistry, and the nonlinear dynamics of complex systems.

Emergence results in the creation of novelty, and this novelty is often qualitatively different from the phenomena out of which it emerged.

p 274 At all levels of life, beginning with the simplest cell, mind and matter, process and structure, are inseparably connected. For the first time, we have a scientific theory that unifies mind, matter, and life.

p 303 ... most scientists tend to think of a pattern of organization as an idea abstracted from matter, rather than a generative force ... The essential characteristic that distinguishes living from nonliving systems— autopoiesis—is not a property of matter, nor a special 'vital force.' It is a specific pattern of relationships among chemical processes ... All these cognitive phenomena are nonmaterial, but they are embodied.

p 318 A machine can be controlled: a living system can only be disturbed.

p 319 The constant generation of novelty—'nature's creative advance'—as the philosopher A. N. Whitehead called it—is a key property of all living systems.

p 321 ... organizations that are truly alive will be able to flourish only when we change our economic system so that it becomes life-enhancing rather than life-destroying.

p 328 ... there is a mental dimension in every illness, even if it often lies in the realm of the unconscious.

p 338 The health revolution goes hand in hand with a worldwide renaissance of sustainable, community-oriented agriculture, based on the recognition of the fundamental interdependence between a healthy soil, healthy individuals, and healthy communities.

p 342 One of the great challenges of our time is to build and nurture sustainable communities, and to do so we can learn many lessons from ecosystems, because ecosystems are, in fact, communities of plants, animals and microorganisms that have sustained life for billions of years.

p 354 A major clash between economics and ecology derives from the fact that nature is cyclical, whereas our industrial systems are linear.

p 355 Partnership is an essential characteristic of sustainable communities. The cyclical exchanges of energy and resources in an ecosystem are sustained by pervasive cooperation.

Sustainability is not an individual property but a property of an entire web of relationships. It always involves a whole community. The is the profound lesson we need to learn from nature. The way to sustain life is to build and nurture community.

p 363 The fundamental dilemma underlying the major problems of our time seems to be the illusion that unlimited growth is possible on a finite planet.

p 437 ... life science corporations ... have ... a narrow understanding of life, based on the erroneous belief that nature can be subjected to human control. This ignores the self-generating and self-organizing dynamic that is the very essence of life and instead redefines living organisms as machines that can be managed from outside, patented, and sold as industrial resources. Thus, life itself has become the unltimate commodity.

p 446 From the perspective of eco-design, it makes no sense to own these products and to throw them away at the end of their useful lives. It makes much more sense to buy their services—*that is, to lease or rent them. Ownership would be retained by the manufacturer, and when one had finished using a product, or wanted to upgrade to a newer version, the manufacturer would take the product back, break it down into its basic components—'the technical nutrients'—and use them in the assembly of new products, or sell them to other businesses. The resulting economy would no longer be based on the ownership of goods but would be an economy of service and flow. Industrial raw materials and technical components would continually cycle between manufacturers and users, as they would between different industries.*

MARY MIDGLEY

After spending 50 years of my life in other countries (and continents), I returned to the UK at the end of 2008. I was 79, and was carrying all my worldly possessions in 8 second-hand suitcases.

In many ways, it was like moving once again to a new country. In my youth, I had been based in London. Now, I was in Newcastle upon Tyne. But I spent my first month renting a spare room from a philosophical celebrity, Mary Midgley. This was long enough to complete my reading of her first book, *Beast and Man.*

It was a great privilege to be able to read an important book and discuss it with the author on a daily basis while reading it.

Mary's views were so consonant with my own that I almost became a disciple of hers. We both saw the importance of Charles Darwin's statement: 'We humans differ from other animals in degree, but not kind.' We both agreed that humans are animals. But perhaps I take the implications further than MM ever did.

If we differ only in *degree,* then *every* aspect of our human personality must be reflected to some degree in our domesticated and wild animals—on land, sea, and in the air. My pet dog is just as surely a person as I am. When a couple of geese behave as if they are in love, they *are* in love. Crows have a sense of humour like us (or at least a sense of fun). Dolphins feel sorry for us, with our poor swimming skills. Humans are not the only ones that have ideas, even original ideas—and act on them.

It's true that humans are the only *linguistic* animal. Language was the key tool that unlocked all the other secrets and enabled us to build the artificial world of civilization. We thought *it* was a better, superior world. Therefore, *we* must be superior beings. But are we really?

The linguistic animal thought it was making the world a far better place for itself. Inadvertently, it was making the world a much worse place for other animals, and was driving many species to extinction. Its militaristic culture now threatens nuclear winter and climate breakdown.

We have yet to prove that the gift of language, along with all that it enabled, was to our ultimate advantage, or that it was of benefit to life on earth.

PAUL JONES

There are two universities in Newcastle. Their campuses lie side by side. Both have departments of Architecture and one has a department of Urban Design.

Even though I was 80 years old when I arrived back in the UK, I still wanted to promote Matripolis, the Ecocity design system I had proposed in my first book, *The End of the Street*. So, I was invited to give a lecture to the faculties of Architecture in both universities. As a result of the first lecture I was hired as an assistant tutor in Urban Design at Newcastle University. This I did for one academic year and have not had much to do with that department since then.

My experience with lecturing at the other university, Northumbria University, was more fruitful. One of their faculty, Paul Jones, was not only awed by the lecture, but bought my book, and read it from cover to cover shortly afterwards.

We became friends, and soon agreed to join forces and submit entries for competitions based on Matripolis. Already by 2010 we succeeded in winning a sort of award in the Integrated Habitats Design Competition. My certificate says:

Runner Up
Awarded to:
>*David Dobereiner*

Project Team:
>*P. Jones & D. Dobereiner*

Project Title:
>*Matripolis*

We submitted entries for two or three other competitions. Paul was very kind and understanding of my situation as a pensioner and always managed to access a university grant, a tax-free sum of money in payment to me as a consultant, because he thought that was right, even though I would have been happy to donate my services to a cause we both believed in.

That cause was called Matripolis, which the Biotope City Online Journal describes as a Green Megacity Infrastructure. Helga Fassbinder further describes it as 'a megastructure free from cars and completely covered by green: a structure of combined terrace buildings.'

I first began using the term Organi-City at the Urban Green Infrastructure Conference, where I lectured in 2015 in Vienna. It was enthusiastically embraced by Blanche Cameron, one of the organizers of the conference. But at that time, I had not thought of giving Matripolis a new name.

⁂

Back home, I mentioned it to Paul Jones as a replacement of our previous name, Matripolis. He disapproved. For him there could be no better term to describe my system than Matripolis (mothering city).

I didn't see Paul for a while and when I did, he told me about his recent lecture tour in east European countries. He was broadcasting my idea (with accreditation, of course) under the heading of Organicity.

I asked: 'but Paul, last time we spoke you disapproved of giving Matripolis a new name. Did you change your mind?'

Paul said, looking a little embarrassed, 'I guess I did.'

RUPERT SHELDRAKE

I never met Sheldrake, although I came close, because I used to visit one of his best friends in Cambridge quite often.

Organicity is:

> 'an *Organic Philosophy* of Life'.

It is underpinned by the book:

> 'A *New Science* of Life' by Rupert Sheldrake.

In my book, I have contrasted the Machinic way of thinking and acting, with the Organic. I then go on to point out the dominance of the former, historically, and especially since the start of the Industrial Revolution. I connect it with the terrible climate crisis we have caused, the emergence of the State with its concomitant war-making powers and the resultant terrible danger of nuclear winter. Equally disastrous has been the mass extinctions, desertification, habitat loss, soil degradation, plastic pollution, the lowering of water tables, and potential destruction of cities due to anthropogenic sea level rise.

My point is a moral critique of the narrow tunnel vision that takes it for granted that humanity belongs to a special category, separate from the rest of the terrestrial ecosystem.

Sheldrake uses slightly different words to refer to the same dichotomy: Mechanistic/Organicist versus my Machinic/Organic, but his point is a slightly different one.

He is concerned to demonstrate the bankruptcy of the currently popular view (at least among agnostic/atheist academics), that everything, including all forms of life, can be explained by the laws of physics and chemistry alone.

But Sheldrake, who is/was a Cambridge University Biologist, points to plenty of evidence from living systems that this cannot be true.

To cite one example, take genetics. It is true that many characteristics in the new born reflect the genetic make-up of its parents. But genes do not determine the *form* of the offspring. We know this because some genes are found to be identical in different species.

Geneticists have discovered there is another factor that must be combined with gene theory to explain the reality of a new life form, some X factor, which they categorize as Epigenetics.

Even Plato, before the emergence of Science as a separate discipline, could see that there must exist Ideal Forms. There must exist, somewhere, somehow, a template, an idea, a memory of the shape of an animal before it can be reproduced.

The architect conceives the plan and puts it on paper. The builder reads the drawing, and builds the actual building from it.

Genes are the builders of the new life form but where is the plan?

Sheldrake proposes the plan is the morphogenetic *field,* using the well-established precedents that modern science has been forced to accept, as in the electro-magnetic *field* and the gravitational *field.*

Sheldrake wrote other books and is still writing. For example:

1988   *The Presence of the Past: Morphic Resonance and the Habits of Nature*
1991   *The Rebirth of Nature: The Greening of Science and God*
1999   *Dogs That Know When Their Owners Are Coming Home*
2003   *The Sense of Being Stared At*

I only discovered Sheldrake's work after completing the main text of Organicity. The reader who has read through thus far will understand my excitement at discovering reputable scientific backing for some of the notions that I had arrived at intuitively.

For example, Sheldrake writes:

> *The results of this research have convinced me that our minds extend far beyond our brains, as do the minds of other animals. For example, there seem to be direct telepathic influences from animals to other animals, and from humans to other humans, from humans to animals, and from animals to humans. Telepathic connections usually occur between people and animals who are emotionally bonded.*

And

> *The universe now looks like a vast developing organism, not like an eternal machine, slowly running out of steam.*

And

> *I also suggest that our own memories depend on morphic resonance rather than on material memory traces stored in our brains.*

And

> *Morphic fields must in some way interact, directly or indirectly with electromagnetic and quantum fields, imposing patterns on their otherwise indeterminate activities.*

And

> *According to the hypothesis of morphic resonance, human beings draw upon a collective memory: something learned by people in one place should subsequently become easier for others to learn all over the world.*

And last but not least

The organismic philosophy *embraces both biology and physics, hence, if morphogenic fields are assumed to play causal roles in biological morphogenesis, they should also play a causal role in the morphogenesis of simpler systems such as crystals and molecules.*

BIBLIOGRAPHY

Andrews, Charles. *From Capitalism to Equality: An Inquiry into the Laws of Economic Change*. Oakland, Calif: Needle Press, 2000.

Albert, Michael. *What Is to Be Undone: A Modern Revolutionary Discussion of Classical Left Ideologies*. Boston: P. Sargent, 1974.

————. *Thinking Forward, Learning to Conceptualize Economic Vision*. Winnipeg: Arbeiter Ring Pub, 1997.

————. *Moving Forward: Program for a Participatory Economy*. Edinburgh: AK, 2000.

Albert, Michael, and Robin Hahnel. *Looking Forward: Participatory Economics for the Twenty First Century*. Cambridge, MA: South End Pr, 2003.

————. *Practical Utopia: Strategies for a Desirable Society*. Oakland: PM Press, 2017.

————. *Rps / 2044: An Oral History of the Next American Revolution*. Hull, Mass: Z Communications, 2017.

Alperovitz, Gar. *America Beyond Capitalism: Reclaiming Our Wealth, Our Liberty, and Our Democracy*. Hoboken, NJ: J. Wiley, 2005.

Arshinov, P. *History of the Makhnovist Movement, 1918-1921*. London: Freedom Press, 2005.

Bacon, Edmund N. *Design of Cities, Revised Edition: The Development of Urban Form from Ancient Athens to Modern Brasilia*. Harmondsworth: Penguin, 1976.

Maksimov, Grigorij P., Bert F. Hoselitz, Rudolf Rocker, and Max Nettlau. *The Political Philosophy of Bakunin: Scientific Anarchism*. Glencoe: The Free Press, 1953.

Bellamy, Edward. *Looking Backward, 2000-1887: With a Foreword by Erich Fromm*. New York: New American Library, 1960.

Berkman, Alexander, and Gene Fellner. *Life of an Anarchist: The Alexander Berkman Reader*. New York: Four Walls Eight Windows, 1992.

Biehl, Janet. *Ecology or Catastrophe: The Life of Murray Bookchin*. Oxford: Oxford U.P, 2015.

Bookchin, Murray. *Post-scarcity Anarchism*. San Francisco: Ramparts Press, 1971.

_____. *The Spanish Anarchists: The Heroic Years 1868-1936*. New York, Harper Colophon. 1977.

_____. *The Ecology of Freedom: The Emergence and Dissolution of Hierarchy*. Palo Alto, Calif: Cheshire Books, 1982.

_____. *The Modern Crisis*. Philadelphia, Pa: New Society Publishers, 1986.

_____. *The Rise of Urbanization and the Decline of Citizenship*. San Francisco: Sierra Club Books, 1987.

_____. *The Philosophy of Social Ecology: Essays on Dilectical Naturalism*. Montréal: Black Rose Books, 1990.

_____. *Anarchism, Marxism, and the Future of the Left: Interviews and Essays, 1993-1998*. Edinburgh, Scotland: AK Press, 1999.

Bohm, David. *Wholeness and the Implicate Order*. London: Routledge & Kegan, 1980.

Bourdieu, Pierre. *Acts of Resistance: Against the Tyranny of the Market*. New York, NY: New Press, 1998.

Brown, David E, Mindy Fox, and Mary R. Pelletier. *Sustainable Architecture White Papers*. New York, NY: Earth Pledge, 2000.

Brown, Lester R. *Plan B: Rescuing a Planet Under Stress and a Civilization in Trouble*. New York: Norton, 2003.

Capra, Fritjof. *The Hidden Connections: A Science for Sustainable Living*. New York: Anchor Books, 2004

Capra, Fritjof, and Pier L. Luisi. *The Systems View of Life: A Unifying Vision*. Cambridge: Cambridge University Press, 2014.

Castells, Manuel. *The Power of Identity*. Malden (Mass.: Blackwell, 1997.

Chambers, Nicky, Craig Simmons, and Mathis Wackernagel. *Sharing Nature's Interest: Using Ecological Footprints As an Indicator of Sustainability.* London: Earthscan, 2000.

Chomsky, Noam. *The Chomsky Reader.* New York: Pantheon Books, 1987.

Chomsky, Noam, and David Barsamian. *Keeping the Rabble in Line: Interviews with David Barsamian.* Monroe, Maine: Common Courage Press, 1994.

Chomsky, Noam, and Peter R. Mitchell. *Understanding Power: The Indispensable Chomsky.* New York, NY: New Press, 2002.

————. *Hegemony or Survival: America's Quest for Global Dominance.* New York: Metropolitan, 2003.

Chomsky, Noam, and John Junkerman. *Power and Terror: Post 9/11 Talks and Interviews.* New York, NY: Seven Stories, 2003.

————. *Occupy.* Brooklyn, New York : Zuccotti Park Press. 2012.

Christ, Ronald J., and Dennis L. Dollens. *New York: Nomadic Design.* Barcelona: Gustavo Gili, 1993.

Clark, John P. *The Anarchist Moment: Reflections on Culture, Nature, and Power.* Montréal: Black Rose Books, 1984.

Clark, Wilson. *Energy for Survival: The Alternative to Extinction.* Garden City, NY: Anchor Press, 1975.

Cole, John. *Global 2050: A Basis for Speculation.* Nottingham: Nottingham University Press, 1999.

Dadd-Redalia, Debra, Steve Lett, and Judy Collins. *Nontoxic, Natural & Earthwise: How to Protect Yourself and Your Family from Harmful Products and Live in Harmony with the Earth.* Los Angeles: Jeremy P. Tarcher, 1990.

Dean, Penelope, ed. *Hunch: Double Dutch.* Rotterdam: Berlage Institute, 2004.

Deckers, Jan. *Animal (De)Liberations: Should the Consumption of Animal Products be Banned?* London: Ubiquity Press. 2016.

Dertouzos, Michael L. *What Will Be: How the New World of Information Will Change Our Lives.* San Francisco, CA: Harper Edge, 1998.

Devall, Bill, and George Sessions. *Deep Ecology.* Salt Lake City: Gibbs Smith, 1985.

Diamond, Henry L, and Patrick F. Noonan. *Land Use in America.* Washington, DC: Island Press, 1996.

Diamond, Jared J. M. *Collapse: How Societies Choose to Fail or Succeed.* New York: Viking Penguin, 2005.

Dobereiner, David. *The End of the Street: Sustainable Growth Within Natural Limits.* Montréal: Black Rose Books, 2006.

_____. *Rosebuds: Gather ye rosebuds while ye may.* Bloomington: Xlibris. 2017.

Dolgoff, Sam, ed. *The Anarchist Collectives: Workers' Self-Management in the Spanish Revolution, 1936-1939.* New York: Free Life Editions, 1974.

Douglas, William O. *Points of Rebellion.* New York: Vintage Books, 1970

Downey, Jillian, and Elph Morgan, eds. *Communities Directory: A Guide to Intentional Communities and Cooperative Living.* Rutledge, MO: Fellowship for Intentional Community, 2000.

Eells, Richard, and Clarence Walton. *Man in the City of the Future: A Symposium of Urban Philosophers.* London: Collier-Macmillan, 1968.

Elgin, Duane. *Promise Ahead: A Vision of Hope and Action for Humanity's.* New York: Harper Collins, 2000.

Feyerabend, Paul. *Against Method: Outline of an Anarchistic Theory of Knowledge.* New York: Verso, 1978.

_____. *Realism, Rationalism and Scientific Method.* Cambridge: Cambridge University Press, 1981.

Fourier, Charles. *Design for Utopia: Selected Writings. with an Introd. by Charles Gide. New Foreword by Frank E. Manuel. Transl. by Julia Franklin.* New York: Schocken Books, 1971.

Fowler, Bertram B. *Cooperatives: Economics of Democracy.* Buffalo, NY: Friends of Malatesta, 1975.

Fraser, Douglas C. *Village Planning in the Primitive World.* New York: George Braziller, 1968.

Fuller, R B, Edgar J. Applewhite, and Arthur L. Loeb. *Synergetics: Explorations in the Geometry of Thinking*. New York: Macmillan, 1975.

Gallion, A. B., and S. Eisner. *The Urban Pattern: City Planning and Design*. New York: Van Nostrand Reinhold, 1983.

Giedion, Sigfried. *Space, Time and Architecture – Fifth Edition*. Cambridge, Massachusetts: Harvard University Press, 1967.

Goldman, Emma. *Anarchism and Other Essays*. New York: Dover Publications, 1969.

Goodman, Paul. *Utopian Essays and Practical Proposals*. New York: Vintage House, 1962.

Goodstein, David L. *Out of Gas: All You Need to Know About the End of the Age of Oil*. New York: W. W. Norton, 2004.

Gore, Albert. *Earth in the Balance: Ecology and Human Spirit*. Boston (Mass.: Houghton Mifflin, 1992.

Greenleaf, Robert K. *The Servant As Leader*. Cambridge, Mass: Centre for Applied Studies, 1973.

Habraken, N. J. *Supports: an Alternative to Mass Housing*. London: The Architectural Press, 1972.

Hartmann, Thom. *The Last Hours of Ancient Sunlight: The Fate of the World and What We Can Do Before It's Too Late*. New York: Three Rivers Press, 2004.

Hawken, Paul. *The Ecology of Commerce: A Declaration of Sustainability*. New York, NY: Harper Collins Publishers, 1993.

Hemenway, Toby. *Gaia's Garden: A Guide to Home-Scale Permaculture*. White River Junction, Vt: Chelsea Green Pub. Co, 2001.

Hinton, William. *Fanshen: A Documentary of Revolution in a Chinese Village*. New York: Vintage Books, 1966.

Jacobs, Jane. *The Death and Life of Great American Cities*. New York: Vintage Books, 1961.

———. *Dark Age Ahead*. New York: Random House, 2004.

Jencks, Charles. *Heteropolis: Los Angeles, the Riots and the Strange Beauty of Hetero-Architecture*. London: Academy Editions, 1993.

Joseph, Lawrence E. *Gaia: The Growth of an Idea.* New York: St. Martin's Press, 1990.

Koenigsberger, Otto H. *Manual of Tropical Housing and Building.* London: Longman, 1973.

Korten, David C. *The Post-Corporate World: Life After Capitalism.* San Francisco: Berrett-Koehler, 1999.

Kropotkin, Petr, and Martin A. Miller. *Selected Writings on Anarchism and Revolution: With an Introd.* Cambridge, Mass: MIT Press, 1970.

Kropotkin, Petr, and Thomas H. Huxley. *Mutual Aid. and "the Struggle for Existence": A Factor of Evolution.* Boston, Mass: Porter Sargent Publishers, 1971.

Kropotkin, Petr, and George Woodcock. *Fields, Factories, and Workshops.* Montréal: Black Rose Books, 1994.

Kropotkin, Petr, and George Woodcock. *Evolution and Environment.* Montréal: Black Rose Books, 1995.

Lappé, Frances M, and Joseph Collins. *Now We Can Speak: A Journey Through the New Nicaragua.* San Francisco, CA: Institute for Food and Development Policy, 1982.

Leiber, Justin. *Noam Chomsky: A Philosophic Overview.* New York: St. Martin's Press, 1975.

Linn, Karl. *Building Commons and Community.* Oakland: New Village Press, 2007.

Lissitzky, Eleazar M, and Eric Dluhosch. *Russia: An Architecture for World Revolution.* Cambridge, Mass: MIT Press, 1984.

March, Lionel, and Philip Steadman. *The Geometry of Environment: An Introduction to Spatial Organization in Design.* London: RIBA Publ, 1971.

Marcuse, Herbert. *The Obsolescence of Psychoanalysis.* Chicago: Black Swan Press, 1970.

————. *Counter-revolution and Revolt.* Boston: Beacon Press, 1972.

McDonaugh, William. *The Hanover Principles: Design for Sustainability.* Charlottesville: William McDonaugh & Partners. 1992.

McDonough, William, and Michael Braungart. *Cradle to Cradle: Remaking the Way We Make Things.* New York: North Point Press, 2002.

McHarg, Ian L. *Design with Nature.* Garden City, NY: Doubleday/ Natural history Press, 1969.

McPherson, E. G. *Energy-conserving Site Design.* Washington, DC: American Society of Landscape Architects, 1984.

Meadows, Donella H., Dennis L. Meadows, and Jorgen Randers. *Limits to Growth: The 30-Year Update.* White River Junction, Vt: Chelsea Green Publishing, 2004.

Mitchell, William J. *E-topia: Urban Life, Jim - but Not As We Know It.* Cambridge, Mass: The MIT Press, 2000.

Midgley, Mary. *Beast and Man: The Roots of Human Nature.* Hassocks: The Harvester Press, 1978.

————. *Animals and Why They Matter.* Athens: Univ. of Georgia Press, 1983.

————. *Evolution As a Religion.* London: Routledge, 2002.

————. *What Is Philosophy For?* London: Bloomsbury Academic, 2018.

Moore, Barrington. *Social Origins of Dictatorship and Democracy.* Boston: Beacon Press, 1966.

Morrison, Roy. *Ecological Democracy.* Boston: South End Press, 1995.

Mostafavi, Mohsen, and Ciro Najle. *Landscape Urbanism: A Manual for the Machinic Landscape.* London: Architectural Association Publications, 2003.

Mumford, Lewis. *The City in History: Its Origins Its Transformations, and Its Prospects.* New York: Harcourt, Brace & World, 1961.

Newman, Peter, and Jeffrey R. Kenworthy. *Sustainability and Cities: Overcoming Automobile Dependence.* Washington: Island Press, 1999.

Ollman, Bertell, and Karl Marx. *Alienation. Marx's Conception of Man in Capitalist Society.* Cambridge: University Press, 1973.

Marx, Karl, Joseph J. O'Malley, and Richard A. Davis. *Marx: Early Political Writings = Selections. English. 1994.* Cambridge: Cambridge University Press, 1994.

Oosterhuis, Kas. *Hyperbodies: Toward an E-Motive Architecture.* Basel: Birkhäuser, 2003.

Paine, Thomas. *The Age of Reason, Being an Investigation of True and Fabulous Theology.* New York: Thomas Paine Foundation, n.d..

Pannekoek, Anton. *Workers Councils.* Cambridge: Root & Branch, 1970.

Pretty, Jules. *Agri-culture: Reconnecting People, Land and Nature.* London: Earthscan, 2002.

Read, Herbert. *The Meaning of Art.* Harmondsworth: Penguin Books, 1966.

————. *Anarchy and Order: Essays in Politics. Introduction by Howard Zinn.* Boston: Beacon Press, 1971.

Register, Richard. *Ecocity Berkeley: Building Cities for a Healthy Future.* Berkeley, Calif: North Atlantic Books, 1987.

————. *Ecocities: Building Cities in Balance with Nature.* Berkeley, Calif: Berkeley Hills Books, 2002.

Reddy, William M. *The Rise of Market Culture: The Textile Trade and French Society : 1750-1900.* Cambridge: Cambridge University Press, 1984.

Ritter, Alan. *The Political Thought of Pierre-Joseph Proudhon.* Princeton: Princeton University Press, 1969.

Rifkin, Jeremy. *The End of Work: The Decline of the Global Labor Force and the Dawn of the Dawn of the Post-Market Era.* New York, NY: Putnam's Sons, 1995.

Rocker, Rudolph. *Decentralization.* Buffalo: Friends of Malatesta. 1970.

Roussopoulos, Dimitrios. *Political Ecology: Beyond Environmentalism.* Porsgrunn: New Compass Press, 2015.

Rowe, Colin. *The Mathematics of the Ideal Villa and Other Essays.* Cambridge, Mass: The MIT Press, 1976.

Roy, Arundhati. *Power Politics*. Cambridge, Mass: South End Press, 2001.

Rudofsky, Bernard. *Architecture Without Architects: A Short Introduction to Non-Pedigreed Architecture*. Garden City, NY: Doubleday, 1965.

Saalman, Howard. *Medieval Cities*. New York, NY: George Braziller, 1968.

Safdie, Moshe, and John Kettle. *Beyond Habitat*. Cambridge Mass: The MIT Press, 1970.

Schuler, Sidney R. *The Other Side of Polyandry: Property, Stratification, and Nonmarriage in the Nepal Himalayas*. Boulder: Westview Press, 1987.

Seale, Patrick, and Maureen McConville. *Red Flag/Black Flag: French Revolution, 1968*. New York: Ballantine Books, 1968.

Sessions, George. *Deep Ecology for the Twenty-First Century*. Boston: Shambhala, 1995.

Sheldrake, Rupert. *The Science Delusion: Freeing the Spirit of Enquiry*. London: Coronet, 2013.

————. *New Science of Life: The Hypothesis of Formative*. London: Blond & Briggs, 1985.

Shepard, Paul. *The Others: How Animals Made Us Human*. Washington, DC: Island Press, 1996.

Smolin, Lee. *The Life of the Cosmos*. New York: Oxford University Press, 1997.

Spooner, Lysander, and J. J. Martin. *No Treason: the Constitution of No Authority. - Lysander Spooner, a Letter to Thomas F. Bayard. with Introductions by J. J. Martin. [with Pref. by R. Lefevre]*. Larkspur, Colo.: Pine Tree Press, 1966.

Starke, Linda, Brian Halweil, Lisa Mastny, and Erik Assadourian. *State of the World, 2004: A Worldwatch Institute Report on Progress Toward a Sustainable Society*. New York: Norton, 2004.

Thirring, Hans, and Murray Bookchin. *Energy for Man: Windmills to Nuclear Power*. New York: Harper Torch Bks, 1978.

Thompson, E. P. *Customs in Common: Studies in Traditional Popular Culture.* New York: The New Press, 1993.

Turnbull, Colin M. *The Forest People.* New York: Simon & Schuster, 1968.

UNEP. *Global Environment Outlook 3: Past, Present and Future Perspectives.* Nairobi, Kenya: United Nations Environment Programme, 2002.

Van der Ryn, S., and Stuart Cowan. *Ecological Design.* Washington DC: Island Press, 1996.

Wallerstein, Immanuel M. *Utopistics or Historical Choices of Twenty-First Century.* New York: New Press, 1998.

Ward, Barbara, and René J. Dubos. *Only One Earth: The Care and Maintenance of a Small Planet.* New York: Norton, 1983.

Ward-Perkins, John B. *Cities of Ancient Greece and Italy: Planning in Classical Antiquity.* New York: G. Braziller, 1974.

Watson, Donald, and Kenneth Labs. *Climatic Design: Energy-efficient Building Principles and Practices.* New York: McGraw-Hill, 1993.

Wells, Malcolm. *Infrastructures: Life Support for the Nation's Circulatory Systems.* Cape Cod, Massachusetts. Malcolm Wells. 1994

Whyte, William F., and Kathleen K. Whyte. *Making Mondragon: The Growth and Dynamics of the Worker Cooperative Complex.* Ithaca, NY: ILR Press, 1988.

Wigley, Mark. *Constant's New Babylon: The Hyper-Architecture of Desire.* Rotterdam: 010 Publishing, 1998.

Williams, A. R. *The Urban Stage: A Reflexion of Architecture and Urban Design.* San Francisco, CA: San Francisco Center for Architecture and Urban Studies, 1980.

Wilson, Edward O. *Consilience: The Unity of Knowledge.* New York: Knopf, 1998.

————. *The Future of Life.* New York, NY: Knopf, 2002.

Wright, Frank L. *The Living City.* New York: Bramhall House, 1958.

Zinn, Howard. *A People's History of the United States.* New York: Harper Colophon Books, 1980.

BLACK
ROSE
BOOKS

the end of the street
sustainable growth within natural limits

DAVID DOBEREINER

Pioneers of
Ecological Humanism

MUMFORD

DUBOS

BOOKCHIN

BRIAN MORRIS

BLACK
ROSE
BOOKS

POLITICAL ECOLOGY
SYSTEM CHANGE NOT CLIMATE CHANGE

DIMITRIOS
ROUSSOPOULOS

BLACK
ROSE
BOOKS

The Philosophy of Social Ecology

Essays on Dialectical Naturalism

Murray Bookchin

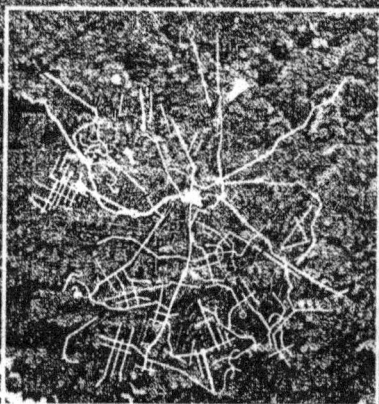

BLACK ROSE BOOKS

URBANIZATION

without CITIES

The Rise
and
Decline
of
Citizenship

Murray Bookchin

THE CITY AND RADICAL SOCIAL CHANGE

edited by ROUSSOPOULOS